The Book of
PSALMS
in
Rhyme

Brendan Conboy
Illustrated by Grant Harman

Come with me now, its journey time.
Come journey through the Psalms in Rhyme.

Published by
Yellow Dog Publishing

All rights reserved.
No part of this book may be reproduced in any form by photocopying or any electronic or mechanical means, including information storage or retrieval systems, without permissions in writing from both the copyright owner and the publisher of the book.

First published August 2021

Copyright © Brendan M Conboy 2021
www.brendanconboy.co.uk

Cover photography – Enrique Lopez Garre
Cover design - Brendan Conboy
Illustrations by Grant Harman

Printed in Great Britain
ISBN 978-1-9169000-6-6

Index of Psalms

Collection One — **Psalms of Creation and Man**

Ps	Page	Title	V's
1	18	The Tree That Thrives	6
2	19	The Coronation of the King	12
3	21	A Shield of Glory	8
4	22	A Evening Cry For Help	8
5	24	Song of a Cloudy Dawn	12
6	26	A Song for Healing	10
7	27	A Song for the Persecuted Soul	17
8	30	Splendorous God	9
9	31	Triumphant Expression of Praise	20
10	34	Shout Against Oppression	18
11	36	You Are My Hiding Place	7
12	37	Awakening	8
13	38	Prayer Changes Darkness Into Light	6
14	39	God Looks Down in Love	7
15	40	Dwelling in Glory	5
16	41	Bountiful Benevolence, Wonderful Inheritance	11
17	42	My Piercing Cry for Justice	15
18	44	Lord, I Passionately Love You	50
19	49	God's Story	14
20	51	Shout for Joy	9
21	52	Because of Your Might	13
22	53	A Prophetic Image of the Crucifixion	31
23	56	The Greatest Shepherd	6
24	57	Here Comes the Glory King	10
25	59	God, Rescue Me, Set Me Free!	22
26	61	Vindicate Me	12
27	62	Courageous Faith	14
28	63	You're My Strength and Shield	9
29	64	Glorious Thunder, Sound of Wonder	11

Ps	Page	Title	V's
30	66	You Miraculously Healed Me	12
31	67	Your Abundant Goodness	24
32	72	A Clean Slate	11
33	74	Shout for Joy, Let it Rip!	22
34	76	God's Gracious Kindness	22
35	78	Save Me	28
36	81	Abundance out of Wisdom	12
37	82	Sing a Song of Wisdom	40
38	86	Before the Throne, I Moan and Groan!	22
39	88	Lord, Help Me!	13
40	90	He Put A New Song In My Mouth	17
41	92	I Can't Live Without You, Lord	13
Collection Two		**Psalms of Anguish and Salvation**	
42	94	He Sings His Song	11
43	96	Your Faithful Guiding Light	5
44	97	Was And Is And Is To Come	26
45	99	The Royal Bride and Groom	17
46	102	Allied With God	11
47	103	Praise Our Awesome God	9
48	104	Zion, High and Glorious	14
49	106	You Can't Take It With You	20
50	108	Hear God Shout It Out!	23
51	110	Forgiveness and Cleansing	19
52	112	The Destiny of the Doubter	9
53	113	Corruption and Destruction	6
54	114	Protect Me	7
55	116	Betrayal	23
56	119	In God I Trust	13
57	120	Triumphant Faith	11
58	122	Who Judges the Judges	11
59	123	Deliver Me From My Enemy Stress	17

Ps	Page	Title	V's
60	125	Does God Remember Us	12
61	126	Protection Prayer	8
62	127	Faith Unshakable, Faith Unstoppable	12
63	129	Yearning for God	11
64	130	Destroyer of Destroyers	10
65	131	Creation Celebrates	13
66	132	Praise The Lord in Exaltation	20
67	134	Voices Raise, It's Time to Praise	7
68	135	Victory Song	35
69	139	Desperation Exclamation	36
70	143	Quickly Come	5
71	143	Song For The Golden Years	24
72	146	The Just and Righteous King	20
Collection Three		**Psalms of Worship and God's House**	
73	148	God's Poetic Justice	28
74	150	Your Restoration, For Devastation	23
75	153	A Cup of Judgement and Fury	10
76	154	Awesome God	12
77	155	God Where Are You?	20
78	157	Reflection Instruction	72
79	164	Disaster is Near, We Need You Near	13
80	165	Salvation Restoration	19
81	167	Celebration for Provision	16
82	169	The Moment of Truth	8
83	170	God, Speak Out, Time to Shout	18
84	171	Desiring God	12
85	173	Merciful Restoration	13
86	174	Prayer of Belief	17
87	176	The Spring of Life and Joy	7
88	177	May Your Intent, Save My Torment	18
89	179	Will You Ever Accept Us?	52

Collection Four		Psalms of Our Journey on Earth	
Ps	Page	Title	V's
90	184	The Everlasting God!	17
91	186	Safe and Secure, We Will Endure	15
92	187	Time to Raise, A Song of Praise	15
93	188	The Majesty of Eternity	5
94	189	Vengeance Time, Vegeance is Mine	23
95	191	Everyone Sing	11
96	192	Everyone Surrender, to the King of Splendour	13
97	194	The Lord Reigns Over all	12
98	195	Sing Along to a New Song	9
99	196	God of Holiness	9
100	197	Praise The Lord	5
101	198	Blameless Existence	8
102	199	Sorrow to Joy	28
103	201	The Father's Heart, Will Not Depart	22
104	203	The Maker Cares, The Maker Shares	35
105	206	God's Beautiful Nation	45
106	209	God of Goodness	48
Collection Five		Psalms of Praise and Word	
107	214	The Endless, Relentless, Love of God	42
108	218	A Prayer for God's Help Against Our Adversaries	13
109	219	God, It's Pay-Back Time	31
110	222	My Lord, Messiah and King, My Everything	7
111	223	Praise and Glorify, Lord Adonai	10
112	224	Shout and Celebrate, the Victory of Faith	10
113	225	Generosity of Lord Adonai	9
114	225	Passover Song	8
115	226	The One Only True God	18
116	228	I Am Saved, From the Grave	19
117	230	The Lord be Praised, for Endless Days	2
118	230	Thanks for Glory, Thanks for Victory	29
119	233	God's Word Must be Heard!	176

Ps	Page	Title	V's
120	247	God Hear My Prayer	6
121	247	God Our Protector	8
122	248	Praise for Jerusalem	9
123	249	Mercy Prayer	4
124	250	Glorious Victorious	8
125	250	God's Surrounding Protection	5
126	251	Restored	6
127	252	His Delightful Gifts	5
128	253	The Reward of The Lord	6
129	253	Persecute the Persecutors	8
130	254	Desperate Cry	8
131	255	My Humble Heart	3
132	255	Destiny and Desire	17
133	257	Peaceful Unity	3
134	257	The Night of Praise	3
135	258	Shout Hallelujah and Praise	21
136	259	His Love Endures For Eternity	26
137	262	Captivity Song	9
138	263	Thanksgiving Prayer	8
139	264	Intimate With Me	24
140	266	Petition for Protection	12
141	268	An Evening Sacrifice	10
142	269	Desperation Prayer	7
143	270	Humility Prayer	12
144	271	Thanks For Redeeming Me	15
145	273	God's Greatness	21
146	275	Praise Our True Saviour	10
147	276	We Praise El Shaddai (God Almighty)	20
148	277	Let The Universe Praise God	14
149	279	Join The Praise Throng, Where You Belong	9
150	280	Hallelujah! Praise The Lord	6

I AM AN AUTHOR
The story behind the author and how this book came into being

I left school without an English qualification. Unable to string two sentences together. It's fair to say that I hated writing. I couldn't see the point. I couldn't see the beauty. The beauty that lies in words. And the power. Words are so powerful. They can bring about change. They influence. But how did I change?

Ten years after leaving school I read about Jesus. Not for the first time, but the words that I read came alive. This man Jesus felt real. So, I stepped into a relationship with him. He came into my life and transformed my mind.

Within a year I was writing rap songs, songs with a message. The words would just fall into my head, sometimes in bed or just walking the dog. It was as if a blockage had been removed.

The cover of this book tells you that I am the author of this work. However, that is not strictly true. All of the words written here are inspired and given to me by God. I see myself simply as a conduit, a messenger and his instrument to be used.

Thank you, Lord God, for speaking to me and for

giving me ears to hear and a heart to receive. For giving me tools and gifts, then telling me to use them for HIM, but it nearly didn't happen, all because of one comment.

*****

Writing this book has been an incredible blessing, but it and the other books leading up to it almost didn't happen. I now feel that it is important to include this story in each of my published books, which you will find listed at the back of this book.

My mum died in 2011 and while sorting through her belongings, we found the start of her life story, in her scribbly hand writing. It was only a few pages long, but it exposed her pain and struggles in life. It was inspirational and it planted a small seed in me. I had the idea of doing the same. That idea rolled around in my head for a couple of years, but I questioned it, "How would I find the time to write?" Life was already busy running a charity (see my book, 'The Golden Thread').

Then, in 2013 I shared my thought with a person that I considered to be a friend. I was hoping to receive some encouragement and reassurance that I could do this, but I didn't!

This is how the conversation went:
"I'm thinking of becoming an author."

The response somewhat surprised me, "You couldn't possibly be an author."
I respected this person's opinion so I asked, "Oh, why not?"
"Because authors write 3,600 words in an hour and you could never do that!"

It was said with such authority, such confidence and knowledge and I just accepted it! "Your right, I could never do that!" I knew that my crippled finger would always slow me down, but I now know that no disability should EVER stop anyone from following a dream. This one throwaway comment would delay my writing like a curse. God was speaking to me, leading me, but a massive barrier had just been built and it would hold me back for years.

In 2015 I stepped down from full-time charity work and managed to free up some time. It was then that I pushed the barrier out of the way and I wrote and first published my first book, my biographical story called, 'The Golden Thread'. It felt good to have a book published. I knew that my story could impact the lives of many and to share it was a way of glorifying God, but I still struggled to consider myself as an author, with my 'friend's' comment still echoing in my mind, *"You could never be an author!"*

In agreement, I now found myself thinking, "Yeah,

it's a one-off, a fluke, anyone can write ONE book! It doesn't make you an author!"

That then was that, decision made, I'm not an author and it's time to move on! Yet, God is patient and he had other plans, but it would take another three years before I knew exactly what he would require of me.

In 2018 my kidneys had failed so badly that I had now been on dialysis for two years. We went to a Christian summer camp festival, called, "Naturally Supernatural." It was organized by Soul Survivor and this was our third year of attending. Halfway through the week, during the loud worship time, in the throng of thousands of people, I became angry with God. I sat and I cried out aloud, "O God! What am I supposed to be doing with my life? Have you given up on me? Do you no longer have any use for me? Why have you abandoned me?"

Then, in the midst of the noise and hubbub, I heard him! It wasn't an audible voice; it was like a brain-download. Some may say that it was a thought, but it was more, it originated from a supernatural source! It was so powerful, "You still have skills and tools that I have given you! I want you to use them! I haven't finished with you yet!"

I felt the warming presence of the Holy Spirit coursing through me and I instantly knew that God had heard my cry and he had responded, but I still didn't know what it meant. Skills and tools? Did he want me to continue in youth work? He had equipped me for that role, but now it didn't seem right.

Later that week, a woman that I had never met before was praying for me. She told me that she feels that God hasn't finished with me yet. She had a picture of me walking and said, "I believe God wants you to walk with your Gospel shoes on and that you will be ready to speak the good news of the Gospel."

For a brief period, once again I found myself angry and confused. I tried to explain to her, "I have end stage kidney failure and I'm waiting for a transplant! I don't think I'll be walking far too soon!"

I was bang-out-of-order, yet she humbly apologised, "I'm sorry, I'm new to this and maybe I have it wrong?"

We both returned to our seats, but something caused me to watch where she went. She was four rows immediately behind where I was sat. Now her words were echoing around my head, just like the words from five years earlier had echoed, *"You can never be an author!"*

She had said, *"God hasn't finished with you yet!"* God

had told me the same, *"I haven't finished with you yet!"* Little did I know, but this was the five year old curse being undone, I was being released! *"I have given you tools and skills…"*

My mind raced through my life, "What tools? What skills?" My racing mind stopped in my first year of knowing Jesus and instantly I knew what he was telling me. I ran back four rows to the woman that had prayed for me. "I'm sorry, I need to apologise. God spoke to me through you and I was too angry to hear or understand, but what you said was spot on. I now know that he wants me to write."

In that first year of knowing Jesus, he had given me the gift (tool) and the ability (skill) of rhyming words and I had used it to become a rap artist. That skill had since developed and my writing skills had helped me to develop The Door Youth Project charity.

I could feel the power of the Holy Spirit already forming words in my head and I was so excited! When I went home from Naturally Supernatural, I had the idea to write some teen fiction. I had previously gathered a collection of teen fiction books, which I now intended to read, in order to gain inspiration. Now, as I pawed my way through the books, I came to an abrupt halt, as I once again heard God's voice in my heart, *"I have given you the tools and skills, now use them!"*

I left the books on the shelf, then, doubt tried to have the final word. *"You can NEVER be an author! An author writes 3,600 words an hour!"* Was that true? I decided to Google it and discovered that most authors write 1,000 words in a day. The figure of 3,600 is how many words a copy typist can produce in an hour. I had been cursed and lied to! Now though, I knew the truth and I started to write my first novel. "Issues" was written in just over a month. Then, as soon as it was published, I felt inspired to write, "My Foundation for Life." I had used the skills and the tools, but still struggled to call myself an author (the curse was strong) – *"You can never be an author!"* The fire was fading in my heart and I didn't write anything for nearly another two years (recovering from a kidney transplant slowed me down). Then at the end of my transplant year of 2019, it started to snow and I was once again inspired to write my first science fiction novel. Then, when "The Invasion of the MIMICS" was eventually published, I could at last call myself an 'author'. The curse had been lifted and with it came a full-on release.

Just a month later, I published my poetry book, "Rhyme Time." Soon afterwards, I was in a prayer meeting, when these words came into my head, "ONE GOD – Many names." I instantly had the thought that I had to produce a film (yes, I also make films) with this title. As the film was being made, I also knew that God wanted me to publish a book with the title and so in November 2020 I started to meditate on the many names and titles of God (over 900 in the book). As I wrote my thoughts and life related stories, I could feel God's Holy Spirit presence growing in me. Then, after just three months and halfway through writing the book, he gave me another 'commission'.

'Commission' is the word that I like to use and I see it as **COM**e together on **MISSION** with God. This time, the call was to use the 'base' writing skill that he had given me *(use the skills and tools)* – 'rhyme'. A friend of mine had recently rewritten Psalm 23 as a rhyming poem. I had produced a poetry book and several 'spoken word' films. Now, I felt God speak to me again, **"I gave you these tools and these skills for this time, everything else that you have written was in preparation for this project. Work with me and write the "Psalms in Rhyme."**

I write to bless others and to give God the glory and so I was obedient and did as he had commanded. So in February 2021, I also started working on "Psalms in Rhyme" and it would take over six months before it was published.

The writing was now flowing, like a supernatural river of words. The curse was broken, "I AM AN

AUTHOR!"

Writing two books at the same time is quite incredible and only possible with God in the mix, but as if that wasn't enough, he also gave me my first illustrated children's book to produce, "The Land of Make Believe." He continued to pour other poems into my mind regularly, plus he gave me the first four chapters of the sequel to, "The Invasion of the MIMICS."

Just a few negative words telling me that *'I CAN'T'* had held me back, but I had learnt. Never let ANYONE tell you that you can't do something or be something!

You can find more information on each of my other published books in the back of this book.

If you would like to bless me and support me, as I bless others and give glory to God, please visit my page: Patreon.com/BrendanConboy

Now, I hope that you enjoy the rest of this book and the stories that God has given me to share with you. I pray that he will lead you and show you what YOU CAN DO for him.

The Book of PSALMS in Rhyme

Collection One
Psalms of Creation and Man

Psalm 1 - The Tree That Thrives
[1] Such enjoyment touches the followers of The Way.
For none will march with evil, nor be led astray.
Never seated with the scoffers and scorned or those that fall away.
[2] Satisfaction and gratification, come from lingering in his Word - never disturbed.
Contemplation, revelation, living in the light.
Heaven, 24/7 every day and night!
[3] Upright, stable, always able, as the tree that thrives.
It's God that plants our lives,
by the streams of paradise.
Fruit bearing all our lives,
he will never dry.
Never faint - no restraint,
forever on a high.
[4] The iniquitous are not the same,
blown like dust, no hope of gain.
Thrown into annihilation!
Destined to obliteration!

⁵ No evil man will tolerate, the day of the judged.
No celestial defence, no pardon for the grudged.
All of their deeds will perish and burn.
Never walk in truth with those that have learned.
⁶ So for the virtuous, good, blameless and just,
God shows the way and follow you must.
The wicked are into darkness thrust.

Psalm 2 - The Coronation of the King

Act I – The People Speak
¹ Why do the people devise an uprising?
Their useless schemes are pointlessly despising.
² See the world politicians, rise up make decisions.
Leaders of the globe, united in derision,
opposing God and uncaring,
for his Anointed King, declaring:
³ "Let's unite and break free from the Maker,
forever discard the chains of those greater."

Act II – God Speaks
⁴ God on high, simply chuckles at their foolishness.
Then he ridicules their utter madness,
⁵ with full ferocity of his flaming fury.
They're shaking in their boots,
as he tells them this short story.
⁶ "I placed my King on Zion hill
and did it for my glory."

Act III – The Son Speaks
7 "I'll show you the everlasting reason of God,
the Holy One.
For He declared to me, I'm His beloved Son.
And Dad crowned me his King Eternal.
Today he, became my Father.
8 He told me to ask him for the world population.
For you are my inheritance, each and every nation.
9 He authorised me to care for you and lead,
you can be taught.
I'll break you all like pottery, crushing rising revolt

Act IV – The Holy Spirit Speaks
10 Listen up, rebellious minions,
you nobodies of dominion.
Learn from my tutorial.
There is still time for you all.
11 Serve and adore, your God in awe.
Tremble in his presence, bow before with reverence.
12 Know that he is great, time now you prostrate.
Now you kiss the Son, before rage on everyone.
Remember have a care, his wrath can quickly flare.
You will be blessed, when in him you hide,
shelter and rest, just turn aside.

Psalm 3 – A Shield of Glory

*King David's song
when he was forced to flee from his son, Absalom.*

The Humble King
¹ Oh, my Lord,
there are so many who want to cause me pain.
² Hear how they gossip and defame,
for their own gain.
Slaying in their saying:
"Just look at him now all a quiver,
The Lord God will not deliver."
(Pause in his presence).

The Comfort of God
³ Yet, deep, deep down I truly feel it,
deep within my heart.
You, oh Lord, you are my shield,
protect me from the dart.
Your arms they do embrace,
your glory covers my face.
And all of my being, watch over me all-seeing,
continually continuing.
High you lift my head, when low I bow in dread.
⁴ I cry out to you Lord
and you respond from your holy place.
You send me a Father's grace.
(Pause in his presence)

The Song of Sustaining Safety
⁵ I now lie down, to sleep and recover from my ache.
You sustain me in your safety, until the hour I wake.
⁶ I am not afraid, though my enemies do surround.
Even in the darkness, your glory surrounds.

My Powerful Hero
⁷ I humbly cry out to you:
Arise for you are just and truth.
You will punch them in the face,
smashing every tooth.
⁸ My hero so true, comes to the rescue.
He alone is my true Saviour.
On his people now pours favour.
(Pause in his presence)

Psalm 4 - An Evening Cry for Help
For public worship –
With stringed instruments - A psalm of King David.

¹ Lord God, you are my righteousness,
my uprightness.
I pray, please respond when I confess.
Give me relief from this distress.
Your grace and freedom, on me bless.
² Hark now all you people, explain:
How long will you defame,
then turn my glory and honour to shame?

STOP! Your abusive rudeness, brings me such pain.
How long will you love your fantasies
and fabricated gains?
(Pause in his presence)

[3] Make sure you don't forget that,
The Lord sees you as an aristocrat.
I know he answers when I chat.
[4] Quake in fear, when The Lord is near.
Let your sins disappear.
Lie still upon your bed, in silent atmosphere.
(Pause in his presence)

[5] Bring The Lord your righteous sacrifice.
Your trust you put in him suffice.
[6] Lord, prove them wrong when they complain,
"God can't save us from our pain."
Shine your light on us again.
[7] Fill my heart with joy, at the time of harvest,
over-flowing wine, bringing me such gladness.
[8] Now because of what you've done,
Lord, I lie down in peace.
Then at the setting of the sun,
all fear will have to cease.

Lord, I lie down in peace

Psalm 5 - Song of a Cloudy Dawn
For public worship – For pipes - A psalm of King David.

Morning Cry
¹ Listen Lord, to my cry of passion.
Can you hear me call in a groaning fashion?
² Do you hear me calling, crying out today?
My King and God, ruminate every word I pray.
³ Every morning without fail, you do hear my voice.
My sacrificial words, to you I rejoice.
At the rising of the sun, every day is a new start,
anticipation for your fire, to fall upon my heart.

Justice
⁴ I understand, that you oh God,
do so detest the lawless.
The wicked are not welcome guests,
they do protest, so thoughtless.
⁵ Proud boasters breakdown under your gaze,
you detest their evil ways.
⁶ You terminate the man who knows no truth.
Reject the hypocrite and the uncouth.

Gathering of Love and Mercy
⁷ As for me, you let me in,
through abundant love and mercy.
Refresh me when I'm thirsty.
I enter the immunity, of your sanctuary.
With deep, deep awe,
I bow to you, in worship I humbly adore.

8 Lord lead me in the right direction,
on your promise of perfection.
My enemies I will displace.
You make straight the path before my face,
by your loving grace, embrace.

Gathering of Reprobates
9 They're a bunch of liars, unreliable,
with not an ounce of trust.
Destructive hearts of malice, undeniable
disgust so unjust.
Reprobates deceive the gathering,
into darkened graves,
with the slickness of their ways.
Their smooth talk will betray!
10 Proclaim them guilty, Oh my God.
May their schemes result in them down-trod.
Cast the rebels out; for they against you do shout.

Gathering of the Blessed
11 Fill them all with gladness,
all who gather in your shelter.
No more lives of sadness,
fill their mouths with joy forever.
Protect them underneath your wing,
may they then, rejoice and sing.
Endless joy will over-flow,
from those who praise your name.
Blessed are they as they go, forever shall acclaim.

¹² Lord,
you magnificently bless the man that is upright.
Your favour as a shield, kindness and joy ignite.

Psalm 6 - A Song for Healing
For public worship –
For stringed instruments - A psalm of King David.

¹ Oh Lord, please don't sentence me to punishment.
Don't chastise me with scorching judgement.
² Please have mercy on me in my sickness,
show your gentleness.
Oh Lord,
heal my broken body, falling apart, in such a mess.
³ My mental health is also broken,
how much longer will I wait.
How long before you have spoken,
in trembling I quake, for you to seal my fate.
⁴ Oh Lord, come back to me, deliver me, set me free!
I know that your unfailing love can bring me victory.
⁵ Now from the grave, my life, please save.
I will forever sing your praise.
If I am dead and in the tomb,
I'll no more sing; just darkest gloom.
⁶ I'm shattered, weary and worn in my lament.
My bed is drenched,
with sleepless nights, all my tears are spent.

⁷ I have so many enemies,
they threaten me by the score.
My heart is filled with sorrow and
my eyes focus no more.
⁸ Depart from me you troublemakers.
Leave me now you troubled forsakers!
My mournful sob is harkened now,
by my Lord who hears.
I cry to God, he sees how,
my eyes are full of tears.
⁹ Oh yes!
The God, who heals has heard all of my pleads.
He takes a grip of all my pleas
and provides me with all my needs.
¹⁰ My enemies have all been shamed.
In fear and grief, they turn again
and in their bitterness, lost in the wilderness.

Psalm 7 – A Song for the Persecuted Soul

A passionate song to The Lord – concerning the curse of Cush, the Benjamite", – A Psalm of King David

An Innocent Plea
¹ O Lord, my God, in you I seek refuge for my soul.
Protect me from my enemies,
who persecute and control.
² Only you can set me free, only you deliver me.
Protect me from ferocious lions,

with fearful teeth I dread.
Can you see the giants? Will they rip me to shreds?
³ O Lord, my God,
if I had done all manner of wrong and perverting,
then I would be guilty and persecution deserving.
⁴ If I had done some wrong,
callously, betrayed a friend.
If I had wrongly harmed my enemy,
I'd deserve a just end.
⁵ Then it would be right for you,
to let my enemy pursue.
Let them trample me into dust,
my dignity let them crush.
And if they chose to kill; me then it's my will.
(Pause in his presence)

God of Justice
⁶ Arise now Lord,
may your anger rise up against my enemies rage.
Awaken fury, stand for me,
decree justice, stop the rampage.
⁷ Assemble all the nations, a gathering of relations.
Whilst you return on high,
to the throne of judgement occupy.
⁸ You are the Exalted One, judging every community.
Do me justice,
according to my righteousness and integrity.
Declare me innocent accordingly.
⁹ End it once and for all,
the wickedness of the wicked and impure.

Righteous God,
search the righteous hearts and make each one secure.
10 Your omnipresent presence,
my protection and defence.
For all who cry out to you, your victory is immense.
11 Whenever you pass judgement,
righteousness is revealed.
The strength of your forgiveness, is never concealed.
Even though you're a righteous judge,
it's not every day we see you grudge.
12–13 Now, if the evil don't repent,
your wrath will not relent.
You prepare your sword and bow.
Your fiery arrows now let go.
14 See how the wicked conceive iniquity.
Their pregnancy lacks integrity.
In labour their lies do come forth.
To trouble they do give birth.
15 The wicked man digs a pit so deep,
then falls in, before it's complete.
16 So the pit-digger's trouble recoils instead,
bringing violence upon his own head.
17 For his righteousness and justice,
I give The Lord my thanks.
I sing praises to The Lord, of the highest rank.

Psalm 8 - Splendorous God

For public worship - On a Philistine lute and [maybe] to a Hittite melody - A Psalm of David.

1 Lord,
your name is great and powerful, full of majesty.
People all over the world,
your splendour may they see.
Your glorious presence, pours it's heaven sent.
All earth filled with the fame, of your precious name!
2 Through the praise, of children and babes,
you built a stronghold against enemy rage.
You silenced Satan in a dumb daze.
3 See your skies, of oh such splendour.
Ingenious blaze, of heavens rendered.
When I gaze up at your moon and stars,
I see jewels in their settings from afar.
I know you are; the fascinating artist,
you made it all exist.
But when I see the wonder, resulting from your tasks,
my mind has a question, so this now I do ask:
4 In comparison to your glorious cosmic plan,
why bother to care, for weak, puny man?
5 Yet such honour you have given man,
slightly less than God, it doesn't make sense.
You crown them all with glory,
honour and magnificence.
6 You made them a delegation, over all creation,
a status of dominion, over all of your formation.
Custodians and authority, such is your decree.

Everything subservient, under Adam's feet.
7-8 All animals of the wild, but also flocks and herds,
all the fish, within the sea; in the sky every bird.
Every part of your creation plan,
in submission to mortal man.
9 O Lord, our Lord, how majestic is your name.
Let all the people see your glory
and everything to gain.

Psalm 9 - Triumphant Expression of Praise
For public worship - To the tune of "The Death of the Son."
– Possibly set for Soprano voices - A Psalm of David.

1 I will worship you, O Lord,
as my whole heart explodes with praise.
I will shout about your wonderful works
and marvellous miracles, all of my days.
Exceed expectations in every possible way!
2 I will leap with joy and shout triumphant!
I sing a song for you exultant.
You are God Most High abundant.
3 As my enemies turn in retreat,
they stumble and perish at your feet.
I worship you in their defeat.
4 For you have fought for my reason and right,
defended me, when I could not fight.
5 From your mercy seat, justice for me you write.
With the power of your rebuke,

nations are demolished.
You eradicate their names, no longer be admonished.
⁶ The Lord roared and our enemies were vanquished.
Cast into eternal ruins, their memories vanished.
Displaced, erased; without a trace.
⁷ Our eternal, mighty God, forever lives and reigns.
Judging from his mercy seat again
and again and again.
⁸ He will decide what is right,
for the whole of mankind.
Dispensing justice to us all,
decree judgement as he finds.
⁹ The demoralised can shelter in your strong tower,
a hiding place from trouble, whatever the hour.
¹⁰ May all who know you intimately,
in you forever trust.
They count on you, so don't neglect,
to help them is a must.
¹¹ To our God who rules and reigns in Zion,
we sing praises of your triumph.
May all of the world heed; the glory of your deeds.
¹² He seeks vengeance for the blood,
of his people unforgotten.
He hears the cries for justice,
from all of the down trodden.
¹³ Remember me, O Lord, show me mercy and grace,
humiliation at the hands of those that hate my face.
What life is this?
Rescue me from death's precipice
¹⁴ Save me! Bring me, to the gates of Daughter Zion.

Then I'll sing of my salvation
and praise you for your triumph.
[15] The godless nations slip, into their pit,
they take the hit.
Guilty! Show them no regret;
they're caught in their own net.
Just let them fret!
[16] God has a reputation, justice for the nations.
The wicked dig their pit, into which they slip.
(Pause in his presence)

Remember this:
[17] All wicked will one day plummet,
into death's dark domain.
All who reject and not submit;
in the death pit they shall remain.
[18] He will not ignore, at all, all the needs of the poor.
The afflicted will not perish, have hope forever more.
For God sees it all!
[19] Rise up, O Lord, let not man prevail.
Judge the nations, each without avail.
Force them to quake in dread,
whenever in your presence.
In essence they're misled,
to you must recompense.
[20] Make them tremble in fear before your presence.
Place a lawgiver over them.
Make them know they are puny, frail humans
who must give account to you again!
(Pause in his presence)

Psalm 10 – Shout Against Oppression

[1] Why do you hide from me?
There's so much evil deprivation?
Lord, why are you far away,
in these troubled times of desperation?
[2] The arrogant man discriminates,
oppressing the vulnerable and weak.
May you crush the man that hates,
turn their aggressing against them bleak.
[3] This wicked man does boast and gloats
of his own heart's desire.
Gives credit to himself, but The Lord, he does revile.
[4] This arrogant man, he is so smug, also so aloof.
He thinks he's safe, yet he's deluded,
so far from the truth.
He says: "There is no God to punish me,
I'll do what I want oppress who I see."
[5] They are so successful or so it would seem.
They prosper in their plans and in their petty schemes.
[6] They scoff and boast,
thinking that they're unstoppable.
Mocking all their victims,
believe stopping them is improbable.
Their hardened hearts do stink,
whilst in their minds they think:
"We'll succeed in everything
and never ever face chagrin."
Though he thinks that he will gain,
all he speaks is spoke in vain.

⁷ Their mouths pour out curses, lies and threats,
bring trouble and turmoil, to those that they oppress.
⁸ He waits inside the city and he takes no pity.
He lurks in the shadows all day, to devour his prey.
The innocent he does slay, murders without delay.
⁹ Like a lion in a thicket, he lies in wait.
Seize a helpless victim, as he seals their fate.
¹⁰ Under their savage whacks and cracks,
they massacre the meek.
Watch their victims collapse, in defeat,
in a painful heap, beat!
¹¹ In amongst their stink, this is what they think:
"God will not see any of our actions.
His ignorance brings no reaction."
¹² Arise now Lord and smash them into oblivion.
Remember the humble, helpless and forgotten.
¹³ It's unbelievable how these evil beings,
treat God with such contempt,
believing you won't call them to account,
never an attempt.
¹⁴ But you O Lord, nothing escapes your observation.
You make notes of the devastation, in every nation.
You see the result of their suffering and pain.
Will you free the oppressed again?
You helper of the fatherless,
defender of the powerless.
¹⁵ Crush the controlling power of the evil bullies,
with their oppressive nature.
Hunt them down, terminate their hate,
obliterate their future.

¹⁶ You Lord, are King of eternity.
All will perish in every city.
¹⁷ O Lord,
you know the mess, the hopes of the oppressed.
Strengthen and solace as they confess.
¹⁸ You bring justice for the fatherless.
No more stress, no aggress, no distress,
no depress, no-more-mess.

Psalm 11 – You Are My Hiding Place
For public worship - A Psalm of David.

[1] My well-meaning friends all tell me to run,
fly to the mountains, like a bird, hides from the gun.
[2] They say:
My enemies plan to shoot.
Destroy with slanderous, deceitful fruit.
From the darkness of their shadows,
bring misery that harrows.
[3] If they destroy my truth foundation,
where is righteousness salvation?
[4] Yet, The Lord, is in his heavenly place,
seeing watching every trace.
In an instance he knows every heart.
His heavenly rule will never depart.
[5] He tests the righteous heart, without any debate.
Those that resort to violence,
with passion he does hate.

⁶ On the wicked, rains fire, brimstone and strife.
A burning wind is their lot in life.
⁷ Yet, never forget:
The righteous Lord, in his heavenly place.
He draws the upright to his presence,
to behold his face.

Psalm 12 - Awakening

*For public worship – Song for the awakening of a new day -
A Psalm of David.*

¹ Help! Save us, Lord!
For the faithful are disappearing.
Lack of faith in all mankind, this is what I'm fearing.
² Everyone lies, everyone deceives,
and everybody flatters.
Smooth talk, double-talk and empty chatter.
Where are the ones that matter?
³⁻⁴ The Lord will deal with them as he feels.
The liar's lips shall be sealed.
To those who speak out seeds of doubt.
Their bitter tongues, he will cut out.
They boast:
Their tongues are theirs to command.
The Lord, silences the bragger, where he stands.
⁵ Then The Lord says, "I will ascend,
the poor I will defend.
I'll comfort the plundered and oppressed;

the disadvantaged who groan for rest.
I will rescue the blessed!"
⁶ For every word God speaks is sure
and every promise is pure.
He is faultless and flawless.
Like precious silver and gold, refined seven-fold.
He is the one to behold.
⁷ Lord, protect all those in needy deprivation.
Save them from this evil generation.
Even though they prowl and strut,
⁸ those who are yours, you still lift up.

Psalm 13 - Prayer Changes Darkness Into Light
For public worship – A Psalm of David.

¹ Lord, do you even remember who I am?
In my troubled state; look at me if you can.
² How long must my heart fight sorrowful pain?
How long will my enemy triumph and gain?
It's been long enough, been so tough!
³ Look on me beyond and please do, respond.
Lighten the eyes of my faith, to behold your face.
In this darkness so explicit, breathe life into my spirit.
I will sleep the sleep of death,
without your life sustaining breath.
⁴ Stop my enemies, from making the proclamation:
"I've triumphed over you, in every situation!"
When I am broken,

my adversaries throw a celebration.
⁵ I trust your unfailing love elation
and rejoice in jubilation,
when I am lifted by your salvation!
⁶ O my God, I burst forth in songs of exhortation.
For my strengthened soul, I sing with acclamation.
In excitation, I praise God for amazing exclamation.

Psalm 14 - God Looks Down in Love
For public worship – A Psalm of David.

¹ The foolish mug believes in his heart,
that God is not real.
Is that how you feel?
If this is what you think?
Your corrupt acts are vile and stink.
All full of falsehood; devoid of any good.
² God looks down in love, from heaven above.
He searches for any, who wisely understand,
for any, who want to please and hold his hand.
³ Yet, everyone has wandered astray,
each to his own way.
He examines each and every one,
but finds no good under the sun.
⁴ See the evil doers exploit all of my people, then
ignoring God, as if eating bread, they devour them.
⁵ See them all panic, overwhelmed in dread and fear,
for God is with the righteous, staying near and dear.

⁶ When the wicked evil doers,
oppress them and frustrate,
the people who are most in need,
will find his hiding place.
⁷ I long for Israel's salvation; from Zion it will be had.
When God restores his nation,
Jacob and Israel be glad.

Psalm 15 – Dwelling in Glory

A poetic melody - by King David

¹ Who shall dwell in your holy place,
with privilege to gaze upon your face,
covered in your grace?
² The one who walks a blameless walk,
with hearts of truth and righteous talk.
³ They refuse to slander and keep a score,
and do no wrong to the man next door.
⁴ They regard God with honour,
yet the vile man they despise.
They keep the painful oath, stay firm despite the cries.
⁵ They'll never exploit or abuse, no advantage took.
Always stand firm, they can't be bought.
They never will be shook!
They're set solid, firm and stolid.

Psalm 16 –
Bountiful Benevolence, Wonderful Inheritance.
A Miktam – A poem to record memories - by King David.

¹ O Mighty God, keep me safe.
My trust in you I do place.
² I say to my Maker, my Mediator,
"You are my Lord.
Without you, I have no accord."
³ And he responds,
"My glorious people, who walk upright,
you are wonderfully noble, in you I delight."
⁴ Those who choose another god,
have sadness multiplied.
To meet with them and drink with them,
never satisfies.
Their ways I do despise.
⁵ O Lord, I have chosen you, you are all that I require.
You hold my destiny in your hands, do as you desire.
⁶ As I follow you on the path of your pleasure,
you overwhelm me with abundant treasure.
Bountiful benevolence; wonderful inheritance.
⁷ I praise you for your counsel
of what is right and foresight.
Your whispers of wisdom fill my heart each night.
⁸ You are always with me, at my right hand.
I'm confident and able, in you I do stand.
⁹ My heart and whole being erupts,
rejoicing in affection.
I'm certain, safe and secure, under your protection.

¹⁰ You will not desert me to the realm of the deceased,
nor allow your Holy One corruption or deceit.
¹¹ Now in your presence is fullness of joy.
Show me your path, on which to deploy.
At your right hand, you never destroy.

Psalm 17 - My Piercing Cry for Justice
A heartfelt prayer - by King David.

¹ Lord, listen to me!
My piercing cry for justice, hear my plea!
I'm an honest man, I tell no lie; hear me when I cry.
² See that I am innocent and show me vindication.
Before your eyes, give me your exoneration.
³ You've probed my heart,
in your night time visitation.
I play no evil part,
my mouth void of all transgression.
⁴ Though some have tried to lead me astray,
following your word has guided my way.
I avoid the ways of the violent,
all my days on you reliant.
⁵ Where you have trod, I adhere so humble.
I follow you, my feet never stumble.
Never fall or stray, from your way.
⁶ My God, I call for you to answer as you care.
You turn your ear to me
and hear my heartfelt prayer?

7 Show me the wonders of your love so amazing.
With your right hand, the persecuted you are saving.
8 You watch and keep me safe,
like a child that you embrace,
hid from all harmful things,
in the shadow of your wings.
9 There, protect me from my enemies,
gathered all around.
Safe from the oppressors,
who crush me and surround.
10 Enclosed in their own prosperity,
they close their hearts to all pity.
In swollen pride they speak with arrogance,
cruel and callous, with such exorbitance!
11 With eyes alert, they track me down.
With plans to hurt, they do surround.
They throw me on the ground.
12 Like hungry lions they wait,
I'm the prey that they will face.
They wait, crouching, lurking in their hiding place.
13 Rise up God, confront them,
bring them to their knees.
With your sword rescue me,
from their rage set me free.
14 Smash them down to the floor.
May their worldly life be no more!
Rip them from their prosperity,
in their fair share of eternity.
Rid them of all their treasure
and all their wicked pleasure.

15 As for me, when I see your face, I will be justified.
When I awake, then by your grace, I will be satisfied.
Fulfilled in the revelation, of your glorification!

Psalm 18 - Lord, I Passionately Love You.
For public worship - A song by King David - the servant of The Lord. He sang to The Lord the words of this song when The Lord delivered him from the hand of all his enemies and from the hand of Saul. He said:

1 Lord, I passionately love you.
My strength is now in you!
2 You are my Fortress, my Deliverer and my Rock.
Your protection over me is strong and never stops.
You're my refuge, my Shield
and the Horn of my Salvation.
I trust you, my High Tower of strength,
you are my destination.
3 All I need to do; is to call to you.
You are so worthy to be praised.
I'm saved from the enemy's blaze.
4 In death's entangled rope,
over-whelmed by torrent's destruction.
5 I fear I have no hope,
in the snare of death's obstruction.
6 I cried out to God in my distress,
"Save me from this mess."
In his heavenly temple he heard me so clear.

My anguished voice, full of fear, softly filled his ears.
My deepest sob; to rescuer God.
⁷ The earth trembled and shook,
rocked to the mountain's foundation.
The mountains moved and quaked,
shaken by his angry indignation.
⁸ Smoke bellowed from his nostrils flared.
His mouth spewed fire with devouring despair,
coals blazing, encircling him everywhere.
⁹ He descended out of heaven's drawn back curtain.
To earth he came for certain.
Through thick black clouds no burden.
¹⁰ He charged in a thunderous chariot,
 his steed a cherubim.
Soaring, swooping, on the wings, of the Spirit-wind.
¹¹ He made the darkness his secret place to hide.
Dark rain clouds of the skies, his mysterious disguise.
¹² Brightness of his advance, so frightening.
Break through cloud, with his bolts of lightning.
¹³ His voice sounded as thunder,
amid flashes of wonder!
¹⁴ With fiery arrows he did aim.
Enemy scattered in flaming rain.
¹⁵ You exposed sea beds and the earth's foundation,
your mighty roar, a hurricane of devastation.
¹⁶ From way up high, he knew; what to do.
Reached out his hand, came to my rescue.
Pulled me from calamity, from despair to his pity!
¹⁷ From my enemy he delivered,
from those so strong that I quivered!

Delivered from my wrongdoer,
he is my mighty rescuer.
[18] When I was weak, I truly faced disaster.
When it was bleak, support came from my Master.
[19] Because of his delight for me, he considered me.
Into a spacious, precious place, he delivered me.
[20] He rewarded me, according my righteous integrity,
recompensed for my clean hands of sincerity.
[21] I will keep his commands and never stop.
I'll never sin, or turn from him; no matter what.
[22] I've stayed focused on his decrees,
obeyed everything that he told me.
[23] I've remained upright and blameless.
I'm uncorrupted and shameless.
Pure and secure!
[24] According to my righteousness,
The Lord has recompensed.
Rewarding me with graciousness,
he sees my hands are cleansed.
[25] To the faithful, you show you're faithful.
To the merciful, you show you're merciful.
To the blameless, you show you're blameless.
To the upright, you show you're righteousness.
How we live dictates what you do.
To the loyal, you are loyal and true.
[26] You are pure to all, who are full of pureness.
To the devious and perverse, reveal your shrewdness.
[27] To the humble and innocent,
you bring heaven's deliverance.
The supercilious and proud, are not allowed.

28 You light my lamp, illuminate my sight.
God my champ; turns darkness into light.
Shadows are no more, I see the path before.
29 With your support, through a troop I advance.
Smash through a wall, given the chance.
30 God is perfection!
His Word, tried, tested with satisfaction.
Secure in the shelter of gratification.
There's no other god like you.
You're the God to worship, I know it's true.
You are my rock, my firm foundation.
My life secure, in every situation.
32 Filled in your strength, showered in perfection.
33 I climb high, with feet like a deer.
Stand strong and secure, with you near.
34 You have trained me for the fight,
with weapons of such might.
A bow of bronze I bend.
Into battle I descend.
35 You provide me with the shield of your salvation.
Your right hand gives sustentation.
With greatness, you made me,
inspired for victory.
36 You set me free, from captivity.
Now, I stand restored, set to fight some more.
On your path so wide, my feet will never slide.
37 I pursued my foe and never retreated,
didn't give up until they were defeated!
38 I smashed and crushed them into the ground,
beneath my feet I did pound.

They fled and bled, as good as dead.
[39] Your strength you did bestow on me,
humbled my enemy, below me.
[40] My enemies turned their backs in flight,
silenced them in their plight.
[41] They cried out for help, for deliverance.
Even God refused them a second chance.
He remained silent, in such defiance.
[42] I pulverised them into wind-blown dust,
trampled them like dirt, in disgust.
[43] You granted me victory over every race.
Now, I'm head of the nations, in this place.
Even those I never knew serve and bow at my face.
[44] As soon as foreign rebels, of me heard,
they submitted and obeyed, my every word.
[45] They all lost their hearts.
The bunch of upstarts,
from strongholds now depart.
Their rebellion fades, as they crawl from their caves.
[46] The Almighty lives! My Rock is blessed!
God our Saviour, our exaltation be acquest.
The Saviour of my days; is worthy to be praised!
[47] God is my Avenger!
All people come, surrender.
[48] Who saved me from my foe?
You lifted me from my enemy show.
The violent man, you brought low.
[49] Before the nations I acclaim,
and praise your Holy name.
[50] Victory and triumph he does bring,

to me David, his anointed king,
and eternally to, my off-spring!

Psalm 19 - God's Story
For public worship - A poem of praise - by King David.

His Story in the Heavens
[1] The heavens declare God's glory, this is his story.
The universe makes a proclamation,
of his marvelous creation.
[2] They speak each day after day, in succession.
Night after night, whispering such wisdom.
[3] Silent, without a word, no voice to be heard.
[4] Yet, the whole world can clearly see its story.
God made a heavenly place, in space,
 for the sun in all its glory.
[5] Radiant, like a bridegroom,
exiting his cosmic chamber each day.
Like a champion runner, such an attainer,
burning up the raceway.
[6] He rises at one end of the heavens,
his circuit complete at the other horizon.
The heat of his rays, touch everything and everyone.

His Story in the Word
[7] His Word is perfect, see, our souls it does revive.
His story, trustworthy and sure, makes the naïve wise.
[8] His teachings fill our hearts with joyful delight,

they're absolute and right!
His commands open our eyes,
with pure and radiant light.
So bright a sight!
⁹ Ignore His direction and live in fear.
Follow His instruction and live with cheer.
His Word needs no change,
no proclamation rearranged.
¹⁰ Like pure, precious gold,
that brings me completeness.
Living words, touching my soul,
like honeycomb sweetness.
¹¹ So we, his servants, are forewarned.
We keep these words for great reward!
¹² Without this revelation,
would I know my heart's distractive situation?
Lord, forgive my hidden and unknown imperfections.
¹³ Protect me from my secret sins,
grant them no dominion.
Then blameless shall I be, free of great transgression,
innocent of rebellion.
¹⁴ May the words of my mouth
and my heart's meditation,
be acceptable in your sight,
my Rock and my Salvation.

Psalm 20 – Shout for Joy

For public worship - For the end times – by King David.

[1] May The Lord
respond whenever you face the adversary.
May the name of the God of Jacob,
offer you sanctuary!
[2] From his refuge, may he support and refresh.
May he strengthen you from Zion's fortress!
[3] May he remember and celebrate your every gift.
Never forget the sacrifices on your list.
(Pause in his presence)

[4] May he grant your heart's desire
and fulfill your plans, even under fire.
[5] May we shout for joy and celebrate,
at his victorious salvation.
Shout to God, for his answered prayers and petitions.
[6] With his right hand of victory,
he answers from his sanctuary.
He gives victory to his anointed king, that's me.
[7] Some may trust in horses,
some may boast in chariots.
We will trust and boast,
in the name of God victorious.
His victory is splendorous.
[8] Our enemies fail, do not prevail; perish and fall.
While we rise up, with courage full, we stand tall.
[9] Lord, may the king win without doubt.
Please answer us when we shout.

Psalm 21 – Because of Your Might
For public worship - For the end times –
A poem of praise - by King David.

¹ Lord, because of your might, the king is strong.
Because of your victory, he rejoices in joyful song!
² The desires of his heart, you have provided.
He speaks with his mouth, you give as decided.
Give everything, to the king.
(Pause in his presence)

³ With rich blessings you came to meet,
placed gold on his head as you did greet.
⁴ Life is what he asked for
and you gave it for ever more!
⁵ His glory is great, because of your victories.
You clothe him with splendour and majesty.
⁶ Because of your success, he is blessed and blessed.
Joy and gladness, he tastes; rejoicing before your face!
⁷ For the king knows that The Lord is trustworthy,
because the Most High is love and mercy.
The king is not mistaken, cannot be shaken!
⁸ Your mighty hands have seized your nemesis.
Your right hand sees your foes in a tight grip.
⁹ When you're ready to fight,
you eradicate them in a fiery furnace.
In his anger,
God swallows and consumes them without a trace,
disintegrated, obliterated, decimated from the place.
¹⁰ Their children will be wiped,

from the face of the earth.
Prevent all their descendants from ever giving birth.
¹¹ We see them plot, scheme and fail.
With evil ways against you Lord, they won't prevail!
Conspiracy will not avail!
¹² You will make them turn away,
aim your justice bow and slay.
¹³ Rise up with all might on display!
By your mighty strength, we all sing!
We praise you, Lord, God and King!

Psalm 22 –
A Prophetic Image of the Crucifixion

For public worship – To the tune "Deer of the Dawn" –
A song of torment by King David.

¹ My God! My God! Why have you forsaken me?
So far from setting me free!
Too far to hear my plea!
² My God! Each day I cry, but you do not reply.
Each night I find no rest, no matter I try my best.
³ Yet, you are the Holy One,
enthroned in the holy place.
You live amid, the holy people's shouts and praise.
⁴ Our ancestors trusted you and what you do.
Generations relied on your true,
and you came through.
⁵ You rescued them from their despair,

no shame because they cared.
⁶ But look at me, I'm like a pitiful worm.
People abuse and despise me in turn.
I don't feel human and I just squirm!
⁷ All who see me mock and jeer,
spitting foul mouthed insults with a sneer.
⁸ "Pahaha! He's the one that thinks God is true!
Let's now see if he comes to rescue?
We'll see just how he delights in you?"
⁹ Lord, from my mother's womb, you delivered me.
I've trusted you, even as a baby.
Since the day of my birth; I've been in your worth.
¹⁰ My mother is maternal; my father is paternal.
In you Lord I place my trust, for you are eternal.
¹¹ Don't leave me, for trouble is near.
I have no one to help I fear.
¹² I am surrounded by the bulls of Bashan,
a violent foe, with an evil plan.
They plan to smash me into tiny bits,
to destroy me in a whirling blitz.
¹³ Words spew from their mouths, full of bitterness,
like a ferocious lion, ripping, tearing, so ravenous.
¹⁴ I'm shattered, fatigued, every bone feels cracked.
My anguished heart melted, away like wax.
¹⁵ I'm dehydrated, parched, can't relax!
I need water, I gasp with thirst.
In the dust of death, I'm carried off in a hearse.
¹⁶ The villainous dogs plan my defeat,
with their deceit.
They pierce my hands and my feet.

17 All my protruding bones can be seen.
The wicked stare with a look so mean!
18 They roll the dice and then decide,
my ripped-off garments tossed aside,
then they gamble to divide!
19 Lord, please don't be distant.
Help me! Make me resistant!
20 Deliver my life from the sword.
Save me from the demonic horde!
21 Don't allow the lions to devour!
Save me from wild oxen power.
The enemy comes at zero-hour.
22 I declare your name to my sisters and brothers.
In the gathered crowd, I praise you like no other.
23 Praise God all you who do fear;
who worship and revere.
All children of Jacob and Israel now cheer!
24 For he has not despised; my desperation cries.
His face He would never hide.
He listens and never denies.
25 I praise because of you.
I praise because you show me how to.
Before all who fear you, I fulfill my vows too.
26 The poor and destitute,
will come, eat, and be satisfied.
Seek God and make Him glorified.
May your hearts be immortalised!
27 From the east to the west, south to the north,
never ever forget, return to The Lord.
Every nation, give adoration!

²⁸ He is Lord of every kingdom!
Ruler over all dominion!
²⁹ The rich and mighty come eating and worshipping.
They stand alongside the humbling and dying,
all in the dust, bowing and fellowshipping.
To honour the worthy King!
³⁰ Posterity will serve him in subjugation.
They speak of God to future generations.
³¹ He will be glorified by those, yet to come.
They will all proclaim and shout, "It is done!"

Psalm 23 - The Greatest Shepherd
A poem of praise – by King David

¹ The Lord is the Greatest Shepherd, my number One.
I always have sufficient, through all that he has done.
² He provides a haven, with lush pastures green,
in which to lie.
He walks next to a gentle stream,
with me right by his side.
³ He revives my very being, seeing;
the transformation of his restoration.
I thrive, as he guides,
me on his path of righteous destination.
So I bring admiration, now to his reputation.
⁴ Lord, even when I have to travel,
the deepest darkest gorge of depression,
your authority gives me strength,

with peaceful impression.
So I will not fear, for you are near!
Now as my enemies do fight,
you provide a feast of delicious, delight.
⁵ You lift me, anoint me,
with fragrant oil that's Holy glowing,
and your generous outpouring,
fills my heart to over-flowing.
⁶ In future, whatever happens, I need not worry!
Why would I?
Your goodness and unfailing love pursue me,
until the day I die.
And when my life is through, I'll forever be with you.

Psalm 24 – Here Comes the Glory-King
A poem of praise to God – by King David.

¹ Everything in the world belongs to God.
Yes everything!
And everyone; you, me, every pauper and king.
² He separated water from land, in his creation,
established, according to plan, a firm foundation.
³ Who will ascend The Lord's mountain peak?
To stand in his presence, who may seek?
⁴ Any with a heart that's pure and hands clean.
None who are deceived by false and obscene!
⁵ They shall receive blessing and vindication,
from our righteous God of salvation.

⁶ God of Jacob, they seek your face.
This generation seek him in this place.
(Pause in his presence)

⁷ Lift up your chin and search within.
Lift up the ancient doors so grim.
Now, let the King of Glory in.
This is what you do, he comes through you!
⁸ I hear you say, "Who is the Glory-King?"
The Lord, who is stronger than anything!
He's mighty in his battling!
So formidable, he's invincible!
⁹ So do it now, lift up your chin.
Fling wide you ageless gates so grim.
Here comes the Glory-King!
Time to let him in!
¹⁰ You enquire again, "Who is this King so Glorious?"
He's the Mighty One, battle ready and furious.
Commander of heavens hosts, Lord of Victory.
Yes, the invincible, King of Glory!
(Pause in his presence)

He's mighty in his battling! So formidable, he's invincible!

Psalm 25 - God, Rescue Me, Set Me Free!
A poem of praise to God – by King David.

¹ My God! My life, to you I bring.
² Always there for me, in you I'm trusting.
Rescue me from disappointment and shame.
Rescue me from their triumphant reign.
Let none who hopes in you, ever be disgraced.
When he has his heart with you interlaced.
³ Yet, those who are treacherous,
to those without blame,
may they be struck, with the blight of shame.
⁴ Lord, direct me, show me; guide me on my path.
Lead my life, so you are glad.
⁵ Show me you're true, O God of my salvation.
My hope is in you, in my daily situation.
⁶ Never forget how loving and merciful you are.
O Lord, this is your way since time afar.
⁷ Forget the sinful ways of my youth,
my rebellious ways so uncouth.
Remember to see me in compassion and love.
O Lord, of goodness above!
⁸ You are so good, upright and true.
You show the wanderer what to do.
⁹ Show your ways to the humble.
Teach them not to stumble.
Bring your demonstration.
Show your revelation!
¹⁰ The Lord's ways of love and faith are evident,
for all who follow his covenant agreement.

[11] Though my sins are great,
forgive me for your name's sake!
[12] Who are they that live in God's Holy fear?
Show them the path, on which to adhere.
[13] They will live in prosperity from your hand.
Their children shall inherit good land.
[14] He confides in those, who in him do fear.
His promises he will reveal.
[15] Rescue me, Lord, from the snare,
for you are the only one that really does care.
[16] In my sadness, loneliness and misery,
I need closeness, graciousness, Lord, I need mercy!
[17] Free my heart from all oppression,
 bring me out of depression!
[18] Look at my burden, the burden of all my sin.
The pain of my affliction, I cannot hold within.
[19] See my enemies are numerous,
their hate for me so furious!
[20] Rescue me! Protect my existence!
Shelter me from shame, in your assistance.
[21] Your integrity and righteousness; are my protection.
My hope is in you, my God of perfection!
[22] Rescue Israel from persecution.
Give your people peace and resolution.

Psalm 26 - Vindicate Me!

A poem of praise to God – by King David.

¹ Lord, vindicate me in my blamelessness,
for I trust in you, without regress.
² Try me, test me; see what you do find.
Examine the truth in my heart and mind.
³ I never stop thinking of your love-unfailing,
and walk in your faithful truth prevailing.
⁴ I never sit, with men of tricks,
or mix, with stinking hypocrites.
⁵ I never gather with the iniquitous.
No way, walk with the nefarious.
Their insipid lies; I do despise!
⁶ My spotless hands are full of virtuousness.
I approach your alter in guiltlessness.
⁷ Proclaiming out loud your glorious praise.
Telling all of your wondrous ways!
⁸ Lord, I love your astounding abode,
where glory dwells and from it flows!
⁹ Don't sweep me away with the sinners that scheme.
Don't end my life with the bloodthirsty and mean.
¹⁰ See, their wicked plans devised.
Their right hands are full of bribes!
¹¹ But me? I live a life of integrity.
Redeem me with your mercy.
¹² My foot stands on an even location.
I praise The Lord, in the great congregation!

Psalm 27 – Courageous Faith

*David's poem of praise to God
before he was anointed as king*

[1] The Lord, is the light to guide my way,
my delivering salvation every day.
I shall not fear, as he is near.
The Lord, protects the way I'm made.
There's none of whom I am afraid!
[2] When the wicked come to plot and ploy.
It is they who run or be destroyed!
[3] An army moves now near, their aim is to kill me,
but still I do not fear, your confidence does fill me.
[4] More than anything else,
my desire is to live in his dwelling place.
To rest in his embrace, and gaze upon his loving face.
To be smothered by his glory and grace.
To seek him in his holy space!
[5] When trouble comes, he hides me in his holiness,
upon his rock, in lofty tent of secret sacredness.
[6] Though my enemies surround,
my head be lifted high.
In his tent I sacrifice, with shouts and joyous cry.
I will sing to The Lord, sing praise to magnify.
[7] Hear my cry! Don't deny!
Be merciful to me, please reply!
[8] You speak to me, saying, "Seek my face."
My heart responds, without need of a chase.
[9] Do not hide your face, and reject me in a rage.
Don't forsake me; I need you, till the end of age.

¹⁰ My parents did abandon me, in revile.
Yet, The Lord adopted me as his child.
¹¹ Teach me to walk like you, on a path that's true,
because of what my enemies do!
¹² Don't sacrifice me, to my enemies desire,
in my painful situation, that wicked bunch of liars.
They spout out accusations; I'm constantly under fire!
¹³ I believe that you; do want me to, thrive.
I will see your goodness, while I'm still alive!
¹⁴ I've learnt through my duration of frustration,
don't give up or struggle with exasperation!
Keep on waiting in faith and expectation!

Psalm 28 – You're My Strength and Shield
A poem of praise to God – by King David.

¹ Help me! Lord, my Rock, hear my plea!
Listen! Give me your guarantee!
If your hearing is depraved,
I will go down to the grave.
Without your reply, I might as well die!
² Can you hear me crying out?
For your mercy I do shout.
I surrender before your mercy seat.
I pray Lord, hear me weep!
³ Don't drag me away with the nefarious.
Those hypocrites are so iniquitous.
Talk sweetly to their neighbours, they're such a farce,

while holding evil against them, in their rotten hearts.
⁴ Give them everything they deserve.
Don't hold back, no reserve!
Pay back according to their deeds.
⁵ Since they don't care or believe,
in you and what you have accomplished.
Flatten them like a building being demolished.
⁶ Praise God, who heard my plea! My call for mercy.
⁷ You're my strength and shield,
protecting me from harm.
My heart trusts you, no need for an alarm.
I break into song, jump with joy,
in praise I raise my arms!
⁸ You will be my strength augmentation,
anointed stronghold of my salvation!
⁹ Save your bequest, let none ever fall.
Like a shepherd, carrying, leading, forevermore!

Psalm 29 –
Glorious Thunder, Sound of Wonder

A poem of praise to God – by King David –
for The Feast of Tabernacles.

¹ All heaven declare his majesty!
Give him all strength and glory!
For he is God Almighty!
² Give to The Lord, the glory of his name,
in his splendour and beautiful, holy fame.

³⁻⁴ The voice of The Lord, like an explosion,
moving over the deep, deep, ocean,
with thunderous commotion.
Majesty in motion!
⁵ His shout of thunder, the booming cheerleader.
The sound of wonder; breaks Lebanon cedar.
⁶ The mighty forests do skip and groove.
His deafening voice makes mountains move!
⁷ His thunderous voice is frightening!
He speaks with lightning striking!
⁸ His voice makes deserts a trembling mess,
shakes the wilderness of Kadesh.
⁹ His bellowing voice; makes the deer give birth.
His vocal sensation; brings deforestation,
over all the earth.
In his temple, all fall and cry,
glory, glory and magnify!
¹⁰ Above the flood and deluge roar.
The Lord, sits as King, forevermore!
¹¹ The Lord, gives his people strength.
His peace and blessings sent!

**The mighty forests do skip and groove.
His deafening voice makes mountains move!**

Psalm 30 – You Miraculously Healed Me
A poem of praise to God –
For the dedication of the Temple - by King David.

¹ I exalt you Lord; you lifted me high in hope.
You did not allow my enemies to gloat.
² I called to you, Jehovah-Rapha,
you healed me because I matter!
³ Pulled me from death's door,
look at me fully restored!
Your healing touch did save,
me rescued from the grave!
⁴ Sing to The Lord, you saints of steadfastness.
Give thanks to God, remember his holiness!
⁵ It's only for a moment, we sustain his scorning,
we weep for a night, then rejoice in the morning.
For a night we face the strife,
but his love will last for life.
⁶ I remember saying, when I felt secure,
"I will not be shaken or unnerved!"
⁷ When you favoured me,
I was mountain firm and blessed.
Then when you hid from me, what a mess,
so stressed and depressed!
⁸ So in anguish I cry out,
"Lord, show me mercy!" I do shout.
⁹ "If I were to die, what would be gained?
Will the grave, cry out your name?
In faithful praise, will it proclaim?"
¹⁰ Hear me Lord and show your mercy.

God help! Show your grace for me.
¹¹ Then he responds to all my ranting,
turns my sorrow into dancing.
He wipes away my advancing, sadness,
wraps me in clothes of outstanding gladness.
¹² Now, my heart sings your praises; never silent!
Lord, my God, I praise you forever reliant!
You give me your healing,
and a joyful, blissful feeling.

Psalm 31 – Your Abundant Goodness
For public worship - A song of poetic praise - by King David.

¹ I trust you Lord, you are my hiding place.
You are my shield, protect me from disgrace.
Deliver me into your righteous state.
² Listen to me! Deliver me quickly.
Be the Rock of my victory.
³ Yes, you are my Rock and Fortress.
In your glorious name, guide me to success.
⁴ From the secret trap they laid,
you protect me and save.
You're my refuge and strength; my enclave.
⁵ I commit my spirit into your hands.
My Redeemer, rescue me where I stand,
my faithful God, of high command.
⁶ I hate those with vanity and insanity,
clinging to their worthless idols.

Their lives are full of denials,
but I trust and lean on you, The Lord of revival.
7 I will rejoice and be glad, in your love perfection.
For you have seen my sad; forlorn affliction.
You are witness of my mess; my life's distress.
8 You have spared me from the enemy hand.
Into open space, you did place,
my feet so they have ran the race.
9 When you see my distress, please don't be merciless.
In my anguished grief I sigh, then cry,
with sorrow in my eye.
My body and soul are weak, I feel such a freak!
10 I am so exhausted! My life has almost halted!
I sigh with sorrow, may die tomorrow.
No longer strong; for I've done wrong!
My weakened bones; so frail they moan!
11 "You are useless!" My enemies are taunting.
Even my neighbours treat me with daunting!
When walking down the street,
they flee to avoid a meet.
12 I'm forgotten and misread, treated as if I'm dead.
No longer regarded, I'm broken and discarded.
13 I hear their slanderous plotting,
trepidation by my side.
They plan to take my life that's rotting
and I am terrified!
14 You are my God, I don't deny.
In you I trust, always rely!
15 Your hands hold my life,
my very being, my destiny.

You can remove strife and tormenting relentlessly.
¹⁶ Upon your servant, shine your face.
Save me from gloom, in your glorious grace.
Save me from doom, in your loving mercy's sake.
¹⁷ Free me, from the shame and disappointment pain.
Show your favour once again!
May disgrace fall upon the wicked instead,
silenced in the place of the dead.
¹⁸ Silence the lips of all who have lied,
they're full of contempt and arrogant pride.
The ungodly, chose the wrong side!
¹⁹ You provide an abundance of good things,
a richness of spilling, over-flowing blessings,
for all who do cheer, you and fear.
They take shelter with you near.
²⁰ You hide the generations, in your secret destination,
sheltered from condemnation.
No more bitter accusations.
The name of The Lord is high and blessed.
²¹ In his refuge, I am his guest.
He protected my back,
when I was in the city under-attack.
²² In my distress, I did express,
that I was cut-off from his sight.
Yet, you heard my cry for forgiveness, in my plight.
²³ Listen, now all you faithful,
love The Lord, express you're grateful.
Be true to him and he'll protect.
If you despise, are full of pride,
then you he will reject.

[24] Be strong, take heart you must, it's true.
Belong, now if you trust, he breaks through!

Psalm 32 is coming up next and I have called it, "A Clean Slate." I now feel the need to drop this poem in here, as it talks about how I started a clean slate.

1986 (Never Look Back)

Back in 1986, I needed a fix.
Not talking 'bout chemicals and party drugs.
I'm talking 'bout the greatest spiritual hug.
If we're really honest and
that's the only way to be.
We all have a spirit that needs to be free.
If being spiritual,
makes you think that I am a weirdo,
Then being lyrical,
breaks your stink to an absolute zero.
When I found my fix, in '86,
something inside me changed.
My nature rearranged,
quit thinking I'm deranged.
He changed the sound in the mix,
still don't wear a crucifix.
He changed the script,
watch my lips, it beats a solar eclipse.
So I kicked, the dirty tricks, no more bricks,
on my brother's head.

I got the fix, because He bled.
No more dread,
He is the Bread of Life.
The thread of sacrifice,
I spread the truth like lice,
because He paid the price.
You see, the fix that I had way back then,
still fills me now, again and again.
This fix is the filler of men,
unless you are mistay-KEN
Forget about the way of Zen,
take you higher than Big Ben.
Higher than Mount Everest,
depart the way of treacherous.
This fix is Oh so generous.
This fix's name is King Jesus.
He's the one that frees us.

I got my fix in 86, made my pick
and never looked back.
Into the light, the right and the white,
shake off the shroud of black.
NEVER LOOK BACK

Psalm 32 – A Clean Slate
A reflective poem - by King David.

[1] Blessed is he who is forgiven.
For his wickedness is hidden.
"Forgiven!"
He utters, by blood he is covered.
[2] Blessed is he with a clean slate.
In his spirit deceit doesn't dictate!
[3] Before I confessed, my inner being was a mess.
My life was filled with frustration.
My heart over-flowed with devastation,
in my messed up situation!
[4] Your heavy hand was upon me 24/7.
Lost my strength in the heat of depression,
that was before my confession.
(Pause in his presence)

[5] At last, I admitted my transgressions.
Then said, "Lord, hear my confession."
He did, took away all evil possession.
No more immoral impression!
No more wrong! All guilt gone!
(Pause in his presence)

[6] This is what I now know,
all believers, to God, must go.
Go confess, your revealed mess,
when the storms do over-whelm,
enter his protective realm.

⁷ Lord, You're my hiding place of resilience,
protecting me from my troubled ignorance,
surrounding me with songs of deliverance.
(Pause in his presence)

⁸ Then The Lord replied,
saying, "I will teach you and keep you by my side,
with my eyes, as your guide.
⁹ Don't be like the horse and mule,
with no understanding, they're absolute fools.
They will not come, they just stand idle,
unless controlled by a bit and bridle!"
¹⁰ So, this now is my observation,
the wicked are full of frustration,
sadly heading to damnation!
But go to God, and then come clean.
He'll wrap you in his love supreme,
then boost your self-esteem.
¹¹ Rejoice, be glad and celebrate!
God is kind, to all who say he's great.
Go on, shout for joy and glee.
With an upright heart, you'll always agree!.

> **Don't be like the horse and mule, with no understanding they're absolute fools.**

Psalm 33 – Shout for Joy, Let it Rip!
A poem of praise - by King David.

¹ Let's sing and shout for Joy! Let it rip!
All believers need to have his praise upon their lips.
² Praise him on your guitar, harp or lyre.
³ Sing a new song, with passion on fire!
⁴ Let's sing about his word, right and true.
He is faithful, in all that he does do.
⁵ God loves to see justice and righteousness.
The earth is full of his luscious loving-kindness!
⁶ When he spoke, the heavens were made.
At his Word, stars and planets obeyed.
⁷ At the sound of his voice,
he poured the seas into bowls.
Then he makes a choice,
kicks the deepest oceans, into his goal.
⁸ Now, let the whole earth fear, let all people revere.
Worship our awesome mediator,
our Lord and God, Creator!
⁹ For he said it and it happened,
became what he imagined.
Think, speak, make, resume; his words went BOOM!
Spoke and it was done, one by one!
¹⁰ As he breathes; he scatters the deceived.
The scheming nations objectives,
are made ineffective.
¹¹ The plans of The Lord have eternal foundations,
the purposes of his being filling all generations.
¹² The nation that has God as their identity,

will be blessed by the legacy,
of The Lord of supremacy.
13 The Lord, gazes down from his dwelling place.
He observes the actions of the human race.
14 He watches everyone; underneath the hot sun.
15 The great Creator, our Curator and heart shaper,
ponders our every caper.
The size of his army will save no king.
16 Even the greatest warrior will have no inkling.
They can't be saved! They'll all be razed!
17 Puny human weapons incite no victory hour.
They will never deliver, despite vast power.
18 He is watching those, who in awe do worship.
For they wait in hope, for his loving fellowship.
19 As for death, he offers deliverance,
even famine makes no difference.
In God we have resilience.
20 We wait in hope for The Lord revealed.
He is our hope and our shield.
21 We make the choice, to rejoice.
In him we do proclaim.
We trust his Holy name!
22 May the unfailing goodness
of your love, overshadow us.
For you we wait, in you we hope,
in you we put our trust!

Psalm, 34 - God's Gracious Kindness

A song - by King David - composed when he pretended to be insane before Abimelek, who drove him away.

[1] I will bless The Lord every second,
his praise on my lips 24/7.
[2] When I see your works, I can't help but boast.
May the afflicted hear and rejoice,
from coast to coast.
[3] Come glorify, come magnify,
The Lord, who does hear our cry!
Let's exalt his name together, exalt him forever!
[4] I cried to God and told him how my story goes,
of course he already knows.
Then he frees me from my fears and foes!
[5] Those that look to him are all aglow.
Their face of shame no longer shows.
[6] When I was desperate and full of fear,
I cried out and The Lord did hear.
[7] The angel of The Lord,
came close to listen as I prayed.
He delivered me and now I'm saved.
As for you; he will do it too!
[8] Taste and see that The Lord is good.
You are blessed,
when you shelter in his neighbourhood.
[9] All you holy people; fear The Lord our King.
For all who do fear him, have everything.
Young lions may grow hungry and weak.
But you will lack nothing, if it's The Lord, you seek!

11 Come, children of God and listen with optimism.
If you fear The Lord, I'll share my wisdom.
12 Who amongst you desires a good life?
To live many long days, without any strife?
13 Never speak a bad word, or let a lie be heard.
14 Let no evil, influence how you behave.
Let peace be the thing that you crave.
15 The Lord watches over his children.
He hears their cries, nothing is hidden.
16 He turns his face from the sinners that shout
and pout.
From the face of the earth, he will blot them out!
Not even their name will remain!
17 Yet, when the followers of God,
cry out in their struggle,
he responds at the double, delivers from the trouble.
18 To the broken-hearted, The Lord is near.
Those crushed in spirit, he restores so dear.
19 Even when,
his children are faced with confrontation,
The Lord delivers them, without hesitation.
20 He protects all of their bones,
not one will be broken by stones.
21 As for the wicked, they all shall be slain.
The followers of evil, condemned to slow death pain!
22 The Lord is observant; to rescue his servants.
Rest in his hiding place, you're not guilty!
You're declared innocent and set free!

Psalm 35 - Save Me
A poetic song - by King David.

Part One – I am a fighter!
¹ O Lord, with all your might, will you fight my fight?
Rouse my accusers and the bruisers.
Stop the chatter of the back stabber.
Please fight my fight?
² Put on armour and shield,
protect me on the battlefield!
³ Seize your weapons! War does beckon!
Pursue those who pursue my damnation.
Tell me that you are my salvation!
⁴ May those who aim; to disgrace me and shame,
be turned back in pain, without gain.
⁵ May the Angel of God drive them away!
Like dust in the wind, without delay.
⁶ May their route, be slippery and dark to boot,
with the Angel of The Lord in pursuit!
⁷ Without reason, they set their trap.
Wanting me to trip, fall and snap.
⁸ Bombshell their wicked contraption.
Catch them in their trap construction.
Let them feel the snap, of destruction!
⁹ The Lord, will see me rejoice and excite.
In his salvation, I will delight.
¹⁰ My whole being will exclaim,
"There is none greater than your name!"
See, you save the impoverished and weak.
The rough and tough, you do defeat.

Part Two – I saw it happen!
[11] Men hostile and ruthless; appear as beguile witness.
They rise up and abuse; they wind-up and accuse.
[12] I show mercy, they bring misery.
They steal like a thief; leave me in my grief.
[13] When they were sick, I prayed for their healing,
burdened by fasting and interceding.
My prayers were persistent; returned with resistance.
[14] I displayed my sentiment,
in heavy-hearted bereavement.
Like I'd lost a friend or a brother,
I wept in grief, as if for my mother.
[15] When this poor boy, did stumble and trip,
they ganged up with joy, to slander and rip,
with disdainful lies and betrayal cries.
[16] Like blasphemous mockers at a feast,
taunting, scoffing and gnashing their teeth.
[17] Lord, how long will you allow these damages?
Rescue me from the ravages of these savages.
I am like a feast; to these beasts.
No more rage, help please save!
[18] Then I will praise, you in the great multitude.
In the mighty throng, I worship with gratitude!

Part Three – I am a worshiper!
[19] Don't allow their sneer for one more season.
For they taunt and jeer, without good reason.
Please don't stand by, and watch them wink the eye!
[20] All their hurtful talk is hateful! By the spade-full,
they devise, accusing lies.

To the virtuous, they're malicious.
21 "We saw you do it!" They gloat and shout.
"If the cap fits, you're guilty without doubt!"
22 My God, you witness everything,
in your quickness do something.
You have seen the hypocrites;
don't let them get away with it.
23 Arise and awake! Show me justice due.
Lord fight for my sake and for what is true!
24 Of course you can judge me,
according to your virtue.
When I make, a mistake, don't let them celebrate,
as they do.
25 Don't let them think that they have success,
or to see their victory through my distress!
26 When they celebrate at my pain,
let them be full of shame.
In their ridiculing place,
cover them in dishonour and disgrace.
27 As for my friends, who do embrace,
my righteous good.
Let them dance and shout for joy, as they should.
For they say, "God be magnified, God be glorified!
He is justified!"
28 I will burst with joy and song,
sing your praises all day long.
You are my liberation, God of my salvation!

Psalm 36 – Abundance out of Wisdom

For public worship - A poetic song - by King David, the servant of The Lord.

¹ Like an oracle of God, rebellion speaks of sin.
The message to the wicked; without integrity within.
They see God near, still do not fear!
² They sweet-talk and butter up each other in praise.
They're blinded by their crooked, conceited ways.
³ What spews from their mouths is deceit and lies.
They're devoid of wisdom, surprise, surprise!
All good has gone, hasta la vista, so long.
⁴ These insomniacs, hatch nocturnal plots.
They're conniving in darkness, never stops,
ignorant of the way, iniquity rots.
⁵ O Lord, your mercy is limitless,
higher than your heavenly home.
Your faithfulness, is endless,
reaches beyond the ozone.
⁶ Your virtue is solid, like a mountain steep.
Your discerning wisdom, like the ocean deep.
You care for both man and beast.
⁷ O God, such a priceless thing,
is your love perfection.
Man shelters under your wing,
thankful for protection.
⁸ Your abundant house, is a feast all can bite.
You pour us drinks, from your river of delight.
⁹ With you is the fountain of life.
In your light, we see light.

¹⁰ Lord, continue to love those who are near.
Bless all those that are decent and dear.
¹¹ Don't allow these boasters proud,
to crush me with their shouts so loud.
Though their numbers may dismay,
don't let them push me away.
¹² See the sinners collapse in pity.
Thrown down for eternity!

Psalm 37 – Sing a Song of Wisdom
A poem of praise - by King David.

¹ Don't be taken in by the sinner's attraction
You want what they have, with a jealous reaction.
Don't think that they have every satisfaction.
² Like grass in the sun, they will shrivel and die.
They're apparent success, will say, "GOODBYE!"
³ Trust in God and do good.
Live in his neighbourhood.
Eat faith and truth like food.
⁴ Delight in The Lord, we all require,
then he will give your heart's desire.
⁵ Commit to The Lord your plan.
Trust he'll do, all that he can!
⁶ He will make your virtue in him,
shine as dawn light.
In the mid-day sun, your justice will be right.
⁷ Be still in his presence and pray.

Don't despair when they thrive their way.
They aren't better than you, that's hearsay!
8 Keep clear of revenge and payback
Don't delight in the fight of spite or you will lack.
9 Destruction will come to the vicious malicious,
but trust in The Lord and have blessings auspicious.
10 Just wait a while, there's no denial.
The malicious will be in exile.
You may look, but they won't be found,
11 But the meek will inherit the ground,
and enjoy peace, safe and sound.
12 The wicked all plan; against righteous man,
with stinking sneers and arrogant jeers,
13 but God thinks it's hilarious.
He sees the end of the nefarious!
14 The wicked see the needy and then take aim,
their way, to slay, those without blame.
15 Up then down, like a rollercoaster ride,
their swords will pierce their hearts of pride.
Their weapons lay broken by their side,
then we will hear their cries!
16 It's better to be with God, with a little wealth,
than to be wicked and rich, but nothing else.
17 The power of the wicked, shall be smashed.
For all God's children, his love is vast
18 Everyday God watches the meek
and their good to reassure.
They receive the legacy they seek,
forever it will endure.
19 In the hardest struggle, in times of trouble,

they will survive.
Can you imagine? In days of famine,
you'll still be satisfied
²⁰ The wicked will perish; it is no joke.
Like flowers of a field, burnt up in smoke.
Full of sorrow! Here today, gone tomorrow!
²¹ The wicked make promises, they never keep.
The good man lovingly gives; what he does reap.
²² The blessed of The Lord, will inherit the land.
The cursed are destroyed, right where they stand!
According to God's plan!
²³ The Lord makes firm every step,
of the one who delights in him, without regret!
²⁴ He may stumble, but never fall.
With his hand, God lifts forever more.
²⁵ From youth to old age, I've been around.
God never crushes a good man to the ground.
Even their children eat, safe and sound.
²⁶ They freely lend, generous to the end… the best!
Their children are blessed and bless the rest.
²⁷ If you really want to make sense,
live forever in God's presence.
Reject evil and do what's right; in his sight.
²⁸ God loves to see us walk in his just way,
never ignoring the faithful who pray.
As for the wicked, obliteration!
Even their children face devastation!
²⁹ The meek shall inherit the land, with every city.
In it they shall live for eternity.
³⁰ The mouths of the righteous utter wisdom.

Their tongues speak about a fair and just system.
[31] Their hearts are full of God's ways.
From the path of right, they never stray.
[32] The wicked hunt down the man of God,
like dog eat dog!
Live for the thrill, their out to kill!
But God will intervene, on the scene.
[33] No condemnation, for the godly man.
No damnation, as per God's plan.
[34] Hope in The Lord, stay true.
He will lift you!
You will inherit, in elevation.
The wicked will see annihilation!
[35] I tell you this, as I've seen it before,
I've seen a rebellious man, crushing the poor.
He sucked the life out of the ground,
defeated all that were around.
[36] Then, he died and no one cried.
None could recollect, the man left no effect.
[37] But the blameless man has a different tale,
with a hopeful future, where peace does prevail.
[38] The sinners face destruction.
No future, just obliteration!
[39] God gives his lovers salvation.
He's their strong foundation.
In troubles, provides restoration.
[40] God will deliver them!
Saved from the wicked, who condemn.
For all who do turn from sin,
can seek refuge in him, under his wing.

Psalm 38 –
Before the Throne, I Moan and Groan!
A poetic lamentation of remembrance - by King David.

[1] O Lord, don't be angry, when you see,
my wrong deed. Don't punish me!
No chastisement I plea!
[2] I'm deeply wounded,
by your arrows of condemnation.
Your hand crushes, offering no redemption.
[3] Due to your anger prevailing,
my body is broken, sick and failing,
because of sin, that is within!
[4] Guilt over-whelms and pulls me down.
Such a heavy burden, feeling I will drown.
[5] My loathsome, festering sickness,
because of my pestering foolishness.
[6] It's all my fault! I'm broken in scorn.
24/7 a miserable mourn!
I am deformed!
[7] Every muscle in my back is under attack.
As for my spine, it's far from fine,
so my body resigns.
[8] I'm feeble and weak, crushed to the bone.
My anguished heart does moan and groan.
[9] See my desire, you cannot deny.
I can't hide my tears and anxious sigh.
[10] My heart throbs, my strength has failed,
the light in my eyes, gone so pale.
[11] My family and friends have no affection for me.

They stay away from the infection they see.
12 My enemies now scheme to take my life.
Hunt me, trap me, stick in the knife.
I hear them talk nearby.
They can't wait until I die!
13-14 Like a deaf man, I cannot comprehend.
Like a mute, I have no words to use, to defend
I'm deaf and dumb and feel so numb.
15 I'm hanging on to a rope.
Lord, I can only wait and hope.
For escape, I do wait.
16 So I pray and say.
"Stop them in their delight, at my struggle in my plight.
Make them refrain, from their pleasure in my pain."
17 My nerves are about to crack,
can't take any more flack!
I'm slipping and falling, as sorrow is calling.
Can't take another whack!
18 Now all of my sin, I can't hold within.
Guilt tells me to confess.
No more suppression, of my transgression.
19 Many are my enemies, vigorous and strong.
They persecute and hate me,
though I've done no wrong.
20 I show goodness, they show rudeness,
like they are clueless.
When I do what's right, even more they want to fight.
21 Lord, don't turn away!
I need you every day.

²² Come as quickly as you can.
My Lord; come with a rescue plan.
Deliver me from condemnation.
You're the hope of my salvation!

Psalm 39 – Lord, Help Me!
For public worship - A song of praise –
For Jeduthun - by King David.

¹ I said,
"I will take heed and be on guard.
All wrongful words will be barred.
I won't speak out with disregard.
In the presence of the wicked,
they try to make me trip.
I have to zip my lip."
² I did as I should, not even speaking good.
I remain totally silent, yet my anguish is defiant.
³ My heart burned within,
thoughts bursting through my skin.
In my mouth it grew and grew,
until the words did finally spew!
⁴ Lord, help me to understand,
how short my time is on this land.
I'm only here for the time you've planned.
⁵ The time that you give, is a mere hand size.
Compared to you, my life is trivialised.
I am nothing before your eyes.

Even the best beware, we're nothing more than air!
(Pause in his presence).

⁶ Like a spectre, we live in the shadow.
Like a collector,
gather but don't think about tomorrow.
We make busy and collect, cling to our things.
We never suspect, who will be wanting.
We gather all day long,
watch the grabbers when we're gone!
⁷ Lord, I state my affirmation,
you're my hope and expectation!
⁸ Lord, I need your protection,
save me from my transgression.
Don't make me a laughing stock,
to the fools that do mock.
⁹ I keep my lips zipped, like I'm dumb.
You are behind everything that's done.
I can't complain, so I remain, shtum!
¹⁰ By the blow of your hand, I am overcome.
Remove from me your bane, deliver from the pain.
If you are against me, I'll simply go insane.
¹¹ When you rebuke and discipline, for our sin,
like a moth is swept away with a wave and a spin.
You sweep away all that we hold within.
We're just a breath formed through a grin.
(Pause in his presence)

¹² God help me! Hear my cry!
Please do not deny!

Can you hear my weeping?
I'm a passing guest, that's fleeting.
¹³ Before I die, fill my soul with joy and gladness.
Smile on my success, and make that frown suppress.

Psalm 40 – He Put A New Song In My Mouth
For public worship - A song of poetic praise - by King David.

1 I waited patiently, for The Lord to pass me by.
Eventually he turned to hear my cry.
2 He lifted me, from the pit of miry clay.
He set my feet upon the rock,
where I stand firm every day,
steadying my steps along the way.
3 He put a new song in my mouth to sing,
a hymn of praise to our God and King.
We see and fear him. We put trust in him.
The many in his gathering!
4 Blessed is he who trusts in God,
and turns away from pride.
Then the followers of false gods,
he does turn aside,
never listening to their lies.
5 My Lord and God,
there's many wonders of your hand,
wondrous things that you have planned.
In you, nothing can compare,
with your deeds I speak and tell.

Too many to declare!
⁶ Sacrifice and offering, you do not desire.
To hear and obey is what you do require.
Offerings both sin and burnt.
Wanted? No, they weren't!
⁷ Then I said, "Here I come, take a look.
You've written about me in your book.
⁸ I delight to do your will, O Lord.
My heart is full with your living Word."
⁹ To everyone I meet, walking down the street,
I do proclaim your name.
My lips, I do not seal, your salvation is so real.
It is my attitude, to tell the multitude.
¹⁰ My righteous heart you give, it is never hid.
I declare your faith and salvation.
Tell your loving truth to every nation!
¹¹ Lord, show me your mercy, with no holding back.
May your love and truth, protect me from the flack.
¹² Trouble surrounds me, so vast.
Without you I know I cannot last.
I have more sins than the hairs on my head.
My heart fails, I'll soon be dead!
¹³ Lord, please come quick and intervene.
Please rescue, restore, you know what I mean.
¹⁴ May those who aim to kill me;
know confusion and shame.
May you now fill them, with disgrace and pain!
¹⁵ As for those who scoff and point blame,
may they be appalled, at their own shame.
See them retreat, in complete defeat!

16 Let all who seek, you with passion,
be full of joy and gladness.
Safe within your compassion,
we magnify your greatness.
Saying, "Praise The Lord, we do illuminate!
Praise God for he is great!"
17 Please come to me just in the nick of time.
For I'm weak and needy, far from being fine.
My helper and deliverer, please think of me today.
Please come to me now; come without delay!

Psalm 41 - I Can't Live Without You, Lord
For public worship – A poetic song – by King David.

1 Blessed are those who care for the weak,
for God is there for them, when things look bleak.
Delivers them in a streak!
2 The Lord jumps right in, to protect and preserve.
He keeps them safe from harm,
blessed as they deserve.
3 When they are sick, The Lord will sustain.
Restore them, to good health again.
4 And when I am sick, I cry,
"Lord, have mercy, please heal me, don't deny.
Heal my body and soul within; for I confess my sin."
5 The haters hiss with menace,
"When will he die and perish?"
6 These 'so-called' friends come to visit,

a bunch of pious hypocrites.
They gather information in their hollow hearts.
Then gossip hollow words, like callous upstarts,
poisoned propaganda and sickening slander.
⁷ They are all wicked twisters,
 who imagine and speak in whispers.
⁸ They say,
"He has his just dessert, got what he deserves.
He's sick in bed, will soon be dead.
His life is down the drain, he'll never get up again!"
⁹ Even my close friend wants to see me dead.
The turncoat!
I trusted him and even shared my bread.
¹⁰ Lord, please don't leave, when I'm in such need.
Your grace I need to receive, to help me proceed.
I'll show them! Yes indeed!
¹¹ When my enemy no longer has the upper hand,
I know you are pleased and that is grand.
¹² You hold me in my integrity.
Fix me before you for eternity.
¹³ God of Israel, receive our blessings.
He's undying and never-ending.
So be it! So be it!

They are all wicked twisters who imagine and speak in whispers

Collection Two
Psalms of Anguish and Salvation

Psalm 42 – He Sings His Song
For public worship –
A reflective poem – by the Sons of Korah
(NOTE:
Psalm 42 and 43 were originally written as one psalm).

[1] As the deer pants,
for water from the mountain spring.
So my soul pants, for God's secure covering!
[2] My soul thirsts and longs for the God that is alive.
My greatest desire,
to meet with God, for that I do strive.
[3] My tears have filled me day and night,
as I cry for God's help from my plight.
The mockers scorn me all day long,
saying, "Where has your God gone?"
[4] As I pour out my soul, I recall these things.
In the house of God, I would lead the praise and sing.
In front of the chanting crowd,
the sound of celebration loud.
Under the protection of the Mighty One,
with shouts of joy and festive fun.
[5] Why does my soul feel crushed by oppression?
So deep within, is my heavy depression!
Hope in God, with patient expectation.
I still praise him with great elation.

Despite my so-called mates,
to live before his face, is my saving grace!
⁶ I feel so down and depressed, I need to rest!
Yet, I keep you in my sight,
from the Jordan River to the mountain heights.
⁷ Deep calls to deep, in your waterfall roar;
my deep need, to your deep love and more.
Your weeping waves of sorrow,
carried me to tomorrow.
⁸ Yet, every day
he instructs his flood of loving-kindness.
Through every night he sings his song,
to ease me in distress.
The God of all seeing; is the God of my well-being.
⁹ Then I say to God my Rock,
"Can you remember who I am?
Why do I have the grief,
of the mockers murderous plan?"
¹⁰ The pain of death crushes my bones,
with the constant taunting from my foes.
Jaunting, "Where is your God?
Ha ha ha! There is no God!"
¹¹ I ask in stress, "Why, my soul, are you depressed?
Why my spirit, can you not rest?
I put my hope in God, with great expectation.
I still praise him for the duration.
To live before his face, is my saving grace!

Psalm 43 – Your Faithful Guiding Light

For public worship –
A reflective poem – by the Sons of Korah
(NOTE:
Psalm 42 and 43 were originally written as one psalm).

[1] Please God! Give me vindication,
from this godless nation!
Rescue me, from this wicked generation!
[2] You are where my strength comes from.
So, why have you turned your back upon?
Why must I mourn? Why suffer the enemy scorn?
[3] Send me your faithful, guiding light.
May it draw me to your holy place of delight!
[4] Then, I will go to God's altar,
to God, my joy, without falter.
I will praise you on my guitar.
Play the tune that's in my heart.
My God, my awesome God, you're the best by far!
[5] Then I ask my soul, full of stress,
"Why, my soul, are you depressed?
I put my hope in God, with great expectation.
I still praise him for the duration.
To live before his face, is my saving grace!

Psalm 44 – Was And Is And Is To Come
For public worship –
A reflective poem - by the Sons of Korah.

The Was
¹ O God, we have heard it with our ears,
what you did for our ancestors in yester-years.
² They reminisced of your expurgation,
driving the wicked from this nation.
You destroyed every fortress under the sky.
You gave them homes to satisfy.
You made our descendants multiply.
In your mighty name, you gave them gain!
³ They battled,
but victory wasn't by sword or their might.
Victory came,
through your hand and arm on your right,
through your glorious face shining bright.
Love delivered delight, from the plight!
⁴ You are my God and King,
declaring Jacob's victory!
⁵ Through your power, we push back our enemy.
We crush our foes in your name,
in your name we do gain.
⁶ I don't trust in worldly fire-power,
for my enemy will still devour.
⁷ You rescue us from our enemies,
your victory we claim.
You defeat the haters and cover them in shame.
⁸ And now, in you God, we always make our boast.

Forever praise your name, because you are the most!
(Pause in his presence)

The Is
⁹ Now, you reject us without honour,
up the creek without a paddle.
No more before us go, in the heat of the battle.
¹⁰ The enemy had us beat, and in our defeat,
we did retreat.
The haters' mighty band; plundered us and the land.
¹¹ You gave us up like sheep to slaughter,
scattered us to the four quarters!
¹² You sold us all as diddly-squat,
valued us as not a lot!
¹³ You make our neighbours scorn and despise,
all mocking and cursing our demise.
¹⁴ Our name has become a joke.
They all laugh, every woman and bloke.
¹⁵ Every day I live is chock-a-block with disgrace.
So, plastered in shame, I block my face.
¹⁶ The haters taunt with torrential vile.
The slaters jaunt, with revengeful trial.
¹⁷ Despite the trial, every mile; we still remember you.
Your covenant, have no denial; stick at it like glue.
¹⁸ Our hearts will never turn back.
Our feet never wander from your track.
¹⁹ Yet, your crushing deformation,
left us in desolation.
Your obliteration, covered us in deprivation,
death and devastation!

20-21 You would know it, if we ignored your name,
would only have ourselves to blame.
If we had turned to false deity,
we would deserve all anxiety.
God, you know what our hearts contain.
In you we long, to remain!
22 Every day for you, we are being killed,
slaughtered like lambs, for the thrill!

The Is To Come
23 Awake Lord! Why do you snooze?
Lord arouse! Will we forever lose?
24 Why is your face hidden?
How can you ignore our affliction?
25 But now, we bow; down to the dust we sink.
Our bodies fall, to the grave and stink.
26 Rise up! Deliver us from our wailing,
because of your love unfailing!

Psalm 45 – The Royal Bride and Groom
For public worship –
A reflective poem - by the Sons of Korah.
A love song – To the tune of "Lilies."

1 My heart is on fire, with gallant desire.
From my heart, the lyrics are rising.
This song, to be sung to the King,
my tongue is storytelling,

words rising, spilling, over-flowing.

The Groom
² You are the most tremendous,
the number one man, so bodacious.
Your elegance and grace, flow through this place.
You are the best! You are eternally blessed!
³ Strap your sword upon your thigh,
O Mighty One, so high.
Clothe yourself in majesty, splendour and glory!
⁴ In your magnificence; ride forth in victory.
For truth, justice and humility,
may your right hand achieve credibility.
Everything that you accomplish,
leaves everyone astonished!
⁵ Men are ripped apart, by your arrows so sharp.
Your precision darts, pierce your enemies heart.
⁶ Your throne O God; is everlasting through the land.
Your kingdom-justice, sceptre is in your hand!
⁷ You love righteousness and uprightness.
You hate wickedness and lawlessness.
That's why God, your God,
lifts you over your friends' badness
and their utter madness!
He anoints you, with oil of joy and gladness.
⁸ Your robes exude the fragrant aroma,
of many perfume treasures.
From your ivory palace,
stringed instruments bring you pleasure.

The Bride
⁹ Princesses are women of honour, in your court.
Draped in gold, by your side, is the Queen consort.
¹⁰ Listen daughter, pay attention,
let go of your past situation.
Forget your own tribe and your father's nation!
¹¹ May the King be entranced, by your radiance!
He is your Lord, so bow in reverence!
¹² Wedding gifts arrive,
from those with wealth and power,
royal friends of the Groom, with gifts to shower.
¹³ Within her chamber,
the King's daughter is glorious,
her gown of interwoven gold, is so luxurious!
¹⁴ She glides before her bridesmaids, so stunning,
brought before her Groom the King.
¹⁵ They will be brought with gladness and rejoicing.
A majestic entrance to the palace of the King!
¹⁶ The place of your fathers, your sons will take.
Throughout the land, princes you'll make.
¹⁷ I will ensure your name,
is memorable in every generation.
Always giving thanks, across all of the nations!

**She glides before her
bridesmaids
so stunning
Brought before her
Groom the King**

Psalm 46 – Allied with God
For public worship - by the Sons of Korah
A poetic song to the melody of "Hidden Things"

¹ God,
you're my strength and refuge in which to hide.
When trouble finds me, in you I do abide.
² We will not fear and tremble,
even if mountains are disassembled,
then cast into a watery grave, beneath the waves.
When the earth quakes and shakes, we stay brave.
Though the seas do surge and swell
and the mountains shake as well,
every dell and every fell.
(Pause in his presence)

⁴ There is a river, with joyful streams a flowing.
Flows through the city of God Most High,
God All Knowing.
He sits in his dwelling place a glowing.
His people have delight that's showing.
⁵ God is in his city, safe and never shaking.
God will help her as the day is breaking.
⁶ The nations are in uproar, their kingdoms tottering.
He lifts his voice more, the earth begins dissolving.
⁷ The Lord Almighty, is with us regardless,
the God of Jacob is our fortress!
(Pause in his presence)

⁸ Come and see The Lord's demonstration,

brought to the earth, his desolation.
⁹ Across the whole earth, he puts an end to wars.
He smashes the weapons to even the score,
all bows, spears, shields and more.
¹⁰ "Be still and know that I am God", is his salutation.
"I will be lifted among the nations,
throughout the earth in exaltation!
¹¹ The Lord Almighty, is with us regardless,
the God of Jacob is our fortress!
(Pause in his presence)

Psalm 47 – Praise Our Awesome God
For public worship – A poetic song - by the Son of Korah.

¹ It's time for celebration!
Clap your hands all you nations!
Shout to God with jubilation!
² The Lord Most High,
is awesome beyond imagination!
The great King over all creation!
³ He subdued the population,
under his feet, ceasing aggravation.
⁴ Our inheritance, he mapped ahead of time,
the glory and pride of Jacob's line.
His love for Jake is so sublime.
(Pause in his presence)

⁵ God awakes to joyful astound!

He rises up to the trumpet sound!
⁶ Sing in the street, repeat!
Dance to the beat, repeat!
Let's celebrate; from dawn till late!
⁷ Over all the earth, our God is King.
Come, let's celebrate and sing!
⁸ Our God reigns over all the nations,
on his throne in communication.
⁹ All the servants of the God of Abraham.
Do gather together, every woman and man.
Even kings unite and sing,
praising God for everything.
They come in expectation.
They sing in exultation!

Psalm 48 – Zion, High and Glorious

A poetic song - for the Sons of Korah.

¹ Great is The Lord and most worthy of praise.
In the city of our God, you do amaze!
² The joy of the whole earth; is its beauty in elevation.
He dwells on his holy mountain,
Zion-City, his habitation!
In the north, Mount Zion rising; to our glorious King!
³ This is his holy place, an indestructible citadel.
We know this lofty place, is where he likes to dwell.
⁴ See the mighty kings unite,
against Zion they planned to fight.

5 They felt prepared, not quite.
The vision of God, an awesome sight!
They turned in flight, ran from their plight!
6 They were seized with trembling fright,
unbearable pain of child-birth like.
7 The wind like a beast; came from the east.
They shattered in your grip,
like stricken merchant ships.
8 First we heard and then we saw,
the wonders of the Mighty Lord.
In the city of Almighty God, he makes it secure,
Forever more!
(Pause in his presence)

9 In your temple God, we meditate,
thinking of your love perpetuate.
10 O God, as is your name,
the whole earth knows of your fame.
Your right hand is full of justice.
11 Mount Zion now rejoices.
All Judah praises for your choices.
12 In Zion, go on walk around,
count all the towers that you found.
13 See her mighty defence formation.
Share this information,
with the next generation.
14 For this is our God, the Everlasting.
He will guide us till our passing!
And beyond, into eternity,
through time and posterity!

Psalm 49 – You Can't Take It With You
For public worship - A poetic song - for the Sons of Korah.

¹ Listen up, every tribe,
all over the world if you're alive!
² Listen! I said, ALL.
That's the rich and the poor!
³ I speak wise interpretation.
I have appreciation,
through my heartfelt meditation.
⁴ I will listen to a saying and to the music playing.
Solve the problems I'm surveying.
⁵ Why should I fear, when evil comes near?
When the problems do astound
and deceivers do surround.
⁶ Even the stinking rich,
they have a boasting switch?
⁷ Yet, none of them could rescue their own brother.
None could pay God, the ransom for another.
⁸ The cost of life is too high a price.
No ransom amount will suffice.
⁹ That they should live for eternity,
avoiding death a certainty.
¹⁰ For the wise and the foolish all die, you will find.
Leaving their wealth to the ones left behind.
¹¹ Their tombs become their eternal accommodation,
the dwelling place for endless generations.
Though their land has their names,
in commemoration.
Their name on a grave, no more;

the only thing to show for!
¹² The man who has everything gained,
will not remain.
Man and beast all perish the same.
¹³ For this is the fate of the confident fool
and those who quote their every rule.
They're not here long; then tomorrow they're gone!
(Pause in his presence)

¹⁴ They're all slaughtered like sheep.
Their shepherd shall bring them, forever sleep.
Then the righteous will prevail over them at dawn,
at the break of morn, far from the manor born,
you find their decaying form.
¹⁵ But God will keep me from the grave.
He will choose me to be saved.
(Pause in his presence)

¹⁶ When others become rich, don't be upset,
with their developed houses and other assets.
¹⁷ For they take nothing with them, when they die.
To their riches and splendour, they say, "Goodbye!"
¹⁸ Though they may have the best,
compared to the rest,
and they're acknowledged as being blessed.
¹⁹ They'll unite with the dead long gone away,
never again see the light of day!
²⁰ Those with wealth, but their knowing denied,
like any other beast, they perish, then die!
In a rich predicament, they all die so ignorant!

Psalm 50 – Hear God Shout It Out!
A poetic song of Asaph.

¹ The Lord God, The Mighty One,
calls to the earth, from the rising and setting sun.
² Out of Zion, God shines forth,
perfection in beauty, showing his worth.
³ Our God comes in a deafening sound.
His consuming fire does surround.
His mighty tempest all around!
⁴ To the heavens above now, he does call.
To the people of the earth, he does judge them all.
⁵ Saying: "Gather the covenant people in my sight,
an agreement they made, by sacrifice."
⁶ His righteousness, the heavens proclaim.
The God of Justice; is his name!
(Pause in his presence)

⁷ "Listen my people, I'll tell you my muse.
I charge you now, you are accused!
⁸ Your constant sacrifices, I do accept,
⁹ but your bulls and goats, I do reject!
¹⁰ Every beast of the field is mine,
on a thousand hills, every bovine.
¹¹ Every mountain bird, to me is known.
Even the insects, I do own.
¹² I wouldn't tell you about my hunger,
for the world is mine and every wonder.
¹³ Do I need to eat; the goat and beef?
¹⁴ To the Most High, your promise you must keep.

Show me your thanks, to bring relief.
15 Call on me, when trouble arrives.
When you honour me, you will survive.
16 Yet, to the man in damnation,
God has this conversation:
"What right have you to speak for me,
and claim my covenant decree?
17 For you hate all my instruction!
You ignore me by your rejection!
18 I see your criminal associations,
and your immoral participations.
19 I hear evil when you speak,
see your lifestyle of deceit.
20 You speak against your brother,
and slander your own mother!
21 You did these things, yet silent I remained.
You thought I was the same.
Now I charge and you arraign!
22 This is your last opportunity,
to turn from your iniquity,
or I'll dispose of you, like debris!
No one will come to set you free!
23 To the believing congregation,
your sacrificial gratification,
is a pleasing demonstration.
Your innocent dispensation,
will bring you my salvation."

Psalm 51 - Forgiveness and Cleansing
For public worship – King David's confessional prayer, after the prophet Nathan exposed his adultery with Bathsheba.

David's Confession and Shame
1 God,
show me your loving mercy intervention.
According to your boundless compassion,
blot out my transgressions.
2 Wash away all my iniquity.
Purge my sin and fallibility!
3 My sin fills me with pain and shame.
My sin it does remain,
contaminates my brain!
4 I sinned against you, within your sight.
My evil deed was far from right.
If you treat me like a blight,
I will not fight, do to me as you like!
5 I was a sinner at my birth,
since I came upon this earth.
6 I know your truth in me,
does bring you delight.
So please, make my heart wise and contrite.

David's Cleansing and Purification
7 Purify me within!
Cleansed for a new begin!
Wash me whiter than snow.
8 Glad songs of joy, on me bestow.
Let the bones that you destroyed,

be healed and then rejoice.
⁹ Hide my sins from your face,
blot them by your cleansing grace.
10-11 O God,
create in me a clean heart,
with a new start.
My steadfast spirit, restore,
now and ever more.
Don't take your spirit away,
please stay with me today!

David's Consecration and Dedication
¹² Restore to me, the joy of your salvation
and an eager spirit sustentation.
¹³ Then it would give me pleasure,
to teach your ways to transgressors.
Then the sinner will repent; return from discontent.
¹⁴ Deliver me from the guilt and shame.
The spilt blood has left a stain!
O God, you are my God, my Saviour.
I sing of your righteousness and favour!
¹⁵ O Lord, open my lips, with words to sing.
Your praises, I am declaring,
my mouth gives you an offering!
¹⁶ For no sacrifice; brings you delight.
No pleasure from burnt offerings sight.
¹⁷ An over-flowing joy now you will find,
when I sacrifice my broken spirit and mind.
My broken heart is now contrite,
sorrow and remorse has won the fight.

God, see me with your eyes
and please do not despise.
¹⁸ May Zion have your affection,
and Jerusalem, your protection.
¹⁹ Then in our restoration sight,
in every offering and sacrifice,
you rejoice and take delight.
In love we do what is right!

Psalm 52 - The Destiny of the Doubter
*For public worship - A reflective poem by King David.
Composed when Doeg, the Edomite, betrayed David to
Saul, saying, "David has come to the house of Ahimelek!*

¹ You may think that you are the protagonist.
Yet, you boast in your evil that exists!
You and your lies; a disgrace in God's eyes!
² You're a slick, twister, deceiver,
with only one function.
Your razor-sharp tongue, is bent on destruction.
³ You love evil, rather than good.
You hate truth and love falsehood.
(Pause in his presence)

⁴ The truth, you passionately love to destroy.
Spinning, twisting, distorting words you deploy!
⁵ You see God will crush you to everlasting destitute.
From the land of the living, he will uproot.

He'll grab you from your tent,
to the grave you will be sent!
(Pause in his presence)

⁶ Then the godly will see and fear.
They will laugh at you and jeer!
Saying, "Let's make this clear.
⁷ This man rejected God's strength and strong tower.
He trusted in wealth, smashed people he devoured."
From evil they did thrive; rich from all their lies!
As for me, I'm like an olive tree.
⁸ In God's house, I'm healthy and green,
I'm protected and seen.
I trust God's unfailing love, all of my days.
⁹ In return, I give you public praise.
In your name, all hope will come,
for your name is The Good One!

Psalm 53 – Corruption and Destruction
For public worship – A mournful reflective poem of David.

¹ "There is no God!"
The fool has said, in his empty head!
They're rife with vile corruption!
None good and all dysfunction!
² From heaven above, God looks down in love.
He searches all mankind, to see if he can find,
any who understand, and reach out for God's hand,

³ but none now do accept him, choosing to reject him!
No good they're all corrupt, on a road to self-destruct!
⁴ Why are the wicked so Naïve?
They take from people, all they receive.
Eating them like bread, never ask God, to be fed.
⁵ Yet, there they are, filled with dread and fear.
There was once no dread, anywhere near!
God scatters the bones of the attackers, so unwise,
put them to shame, for them, God does despise!
⁶ O, come salvation, for the Israel nation!
From Zion come forth, your people, God restores.
See Jacob's celebration and Israel's jubilation!

Psalm 54 - Protect Me
For public worship - David's contemplative song of derision - When the Ziphites betrayed David to Saul, saying, "David is hiding among us; come and get him!"

¹ O God, save me by your mighty name!
Clear me of suspicion and all blame!
² Hear my prayer, O God; listen to my Sob!
³ Godless, ruthless people; full of strife.
Rise up with knife; to take my life!
(Pause in his presence)

⁴ God is my helper; surely that is plain.
It is me, who he, does sustain!
⁵ Let the haters, who slander and ploy,

by God's faith, be destroyed!
May they reap what they sow,
and have nothing to show!
6 Lord, I give myself as an offering.
The praises of your name I sing.
My sacrifice I should, because your name is good!
7 You delivered me from all of my trouble.
I've seen my triumph over struggle.
My enemies, you defeat,
I witnessed them be beat!

Having been a Christian for over 30 years, I have attended a lot of different churches. I also belong to a good selection of online Christian groups and set up one, now with 3,000 members. So I have been in contact with thousands of Christians. Sadly, no matter where I go, I find damaged Christians. Christians that are hurting, struggling and recovering. They all have one thing in common, they are all recovering from the same thing; 'friendly fire'! This is the name that I use to describe, Christian v's Christian. Why does this happen? Why do we inflict pain, suffering, grief and betrayal on each other? I wonder what God must feel, when he hears our cutting remarks, when we reject our Christian brothers and when we deceive them. If you have been a victim of this kind of attack, please find the right kind of pastoral support, but also draw strength from this next Psalm

Psalm 55 - Betrayal

For public worship –
by King David - A song of derision, for instruction.

¹ Hear my prayer! O God, listen to me!
Don't hide your heart when I plea!
² Give me your answer, come close by my side.
Hear my moaning, troubled cry.
³ My enemy isn't shy.
My peace they do deny.
With their words they threaten,
anger and suffering, their crushing weapon.
Their enraged roar, they're bent on war!
⁴ My heart is pounding, inside my chest.
Terror seizes me, with a fear of death.
⁵ I am overcome, by the pending gloom,
I tremor before the horror and doom!
⁶ Then to myself I say,
"If only I could fly away,
to the place of peace, I would stay.
⁷ Run and hide in a place so discreet.
No one would seek, me in the desert retreat."
(Pause in his presence)

⁸ To the higher place, I will stride.
From tempest and storm, I will hide.
⁹ Lord, fill the wicked with confusion.
in the divided city of pollution.
They pollute with strife and slander.

So destroy them with your anger.
¹⁰ 24/7 they watch, as a vigilance committee.
Though, the real danger is within the city,
in the peoples' strife and misery.
¹¹ Murder and destruction, on the increase.
Threats and lies, never leave the streets.
¹² But the one that taunted me; wasn't my enemy.
If it was a proud one, who hated me,
I would have had some pity,
I would just flee!
¹³ No! It was you! My closest friend!
My trusted companion, in whom I depend!
I walked and worked with, to the end!
¹⁴ Together we had sweet fellowship.
At the house of God, we worshipped
We joined in celebration,
¹⁵ now, you have darkness and desolation.
May you and all alike, filled with such despite,
find death obliteration; be buried in annihilation!
¹⁶ As for me,
I call to God for salvation, then, it is given.
¹⁷ 24/7 in my distress, I know The Lord does listen.
He will always hear my cry. He will always satisfy!
¹⁸ Though many wish to fight,
he plucks me from the plight.
Without a scar in sight, I'm safe within his might.
I'm out numbered in battle, and the enemy surround.
Though, by your power, I'll be safe and sound!
¹⁹ God will hear me! Wait and see!
God-Enthroned, through everlasting.

God, of faithful unchanging!
He will hear my shout and he will sort them out!
(Pause in his presence)

[20] I was betrayed by my friend and,
without cause or reason.
Whilst friendly shaking my hand,
he was plotting his dirty treason.
He's a promise breaker! A real faker!
[21] His words were smooth and slick,
yet hate was in his eyes.
The hatred in his heart; was cleverly disguised,
while scheming my demise!
[22] So here's what I know,
cast your cares on The Lord, it's the way to go.
Then you'll be sustained, in his hand you will remain.
[23] He watches over his people of devotion.
Never lets them slip, or thrown into commotion.
My enemies sent to the pit, of destruction.
Death for those full of corruption!
I hope and trust in your instruction.
Saved from revulsion and deception!

Though many wish to fight He plucks me from the plight

Psalm 56 - In God I Trust

For public worship – A song by King David – to the tune of "A Dove on Distant Oaks." Composed when the Philistines had seized him in Gath.

[1] Lord, show me your mercy, that I may relax.
My enemies are in pursuit; on my back.
They constantly press their attack!
[2] All day long, they lie in wait,
in their pride, decide my fate.
[3] When fear upon me is thrust,
I turn to you, the God I trust.
[4] My heart fills with God's praise.
In God I trust, I'm not afraid.
Can a man cause my malaise?
[5] They twist my words, one day after another,
their evil plan, to make me suffer.
They ploy, to destroy!
[6] Watching, lurking, they conspire.
My death they do desire!
[7] They are so full of sin!
You cannot let them win!
Through your anger therein,
smash them down and all their kin!
[8] See my misery and keep a score,
see my tears pour,
count them in your bottle store.
[8] You see them when you look.
Do you record them in your book?
[9] The moment that I cry out,

my enemies turn in doubt.
With this it's verified, God is on my side!
¹⁰ I trust in The Lord and I praise him!
I trust in the Word of God and I praise him!
¹¹ In God, I place my trust and confidence.
The things that man can do, has no consequence!
¹² O God, to you I made a vow,
so I offer my praises, to you now.
¹³ You save my soul from death's bite,
kept my feet, on the path of right.
That I may walk within God's sight,
The God of life and light.

Psalm 57 - Triumphant Faith

For public worship – by King David – A memoire song, to the tune, "Do Not Destroy." Composed when he hid in a cave from Saul.

¹ O Lord, from your mercy seat;
show me mercy, I repeat.
Your mercy I do seek!
In you I am sheltering.
Take refuge, underneath your wing.
Until this trouble's passing.
² I cry out to God Most High.
The God of Wonders satisfies.
For vindication and exoneration, I do gratify!
³ He sends help through heaven's commute,

in pursuit, of all that do rebuke.
His love he sends forth, in his faithful worth!
(Pause in his presence)

4 I'm surrounded by these lions
and live with fierce beasts,
with men that have weapons, as their teeth.
Their tongues like sharp swords, without a sheath.
Angry threats, they do breathe; as they do seethe.
5 Lord God, above the heavens, may you be exalted!
Let your glory over all the earth, be undaunted!
6 Before me, they set a trap, to catch me and suppress,
when I was bowed down in my distress.
But nonetheless; it is they that the trap does possess!
(Pause in his presence)

7 My heart, O God, is firm and unwavering.
I passionately sing; beautiful music I am making!
8 Awake my soul; be stimulant!
Awake my stringed instruments!
I awake the dawn with impetus!
9 O God, I praise you wherever I go.
Everyone will hear my worship so.
10 Reaching to the heavens, your love is massive.
Stretching to the clouds, your faith is lavish!
11 Lord God, above the heavens, may you be exalted!
Let your glory over all the earth, be undaunted!

Psalm 58 – Who Judges the Judges

For public worship – by King David –
A memoire song, to the tune, "Do Not Destroy."

¹ Do you rulers ever speak impartially?
Do you judge people with equality?
² No! In your heart, injustice is planned.
You dish out in the land, the violence of your hands!
³ From the day that they are born,
the wicked go astray.
Liars from the womb, it is their way.
⁴ They are poisonous, like a snake of fear,
a venomous cobra, with blocked up ear.
⁵ They will fail to hear the charmer's flute,
despite the enchanter, playing skilfully cute.
⁶ O Lord, smash their fangs,
and the teeth of lions, with their ravenous pangs!
⁷ Like water that flows away, let them vanish.
Smash their weapons, remove their vantage!
⁸ Let them be like slugs, dissolving, melting away.
Like a still born, never see the light of day!
⁹ In the blink of an eye, whether green or dry,
the wicked will be swept on by!
Hit so fast, they could never last!
¹⁰ The righteous will celebrate in their vengeance.
The blood of the wicked,
is their footbath of deliverance!
¹¹ Then all will say, "God judges the judges.
He rewards our loving him and never grudges!"

Psalm 59 – Deliver Me From My Enemy Stress
For public worship – by King David –
A memoire song, to the tune, "Do Not Destroy."
When Saul, sent men to David's house, in order to kill him.

[1] My God, deliver me from my enemy stress.
When they attack, you're my fortress!
[2] Deliver me from evil, again and again.
And save me from, the bloodthirsty men!
[3] See how they lie in wait.
Fierce men; conspire my fate.
Lord, what sin do I make?
[4] I am innocent, yet they're ready to fight.
Arise and help me; look on my plight!
[5] O God of Israel, now awake!
Arise and oppose these treacherous snakes.
Make no mistake! Make these traitors ache,
As you smash and break!
(Pause in his presence)

[6] They return at night, like dogs snarling, growling.
Through the city they go, strutting and prowling.
[7] Rage from their mouths does belch and spew,
slanderous lies, like a sword they strew.
They pursue, with their onslaught,
thinking that, they'll never be caught!
[8] But Lord, you laugh and mock their torment,
amused at their arrogance and contempt.
[9] I wait for you, you are my strength.
My God is my defence!

10 My merciful God, will meet me.
Then over my enemy, he lets me gloat in victory!
11 Don't kill them! O Lord, who does protect,
instead, by your mighty power reject.
Bring them down and subject,
to wandering disconnect!
12 For their mouths of sin and the words within.
Let them be caught in pride,
for their curses and their lies!
13 In your wrath, consume them all,
devour until they are no more!
To the end of the earth, let it be known,
God rules Israel, from his throne!
(*Pause in his presence*)

14 Allow them to return again,
the pack of dogs in disdain.
At night, like dogs they snarl and growl.
In the city they fowl and prowl.
15 Wandering, consuming, here for the thrill of the kill.
They're not satisfied until; they've had their fill.
16 But as for me, your strength will be;
my song of loving glee.
In the morning I sing of your loving kindness,
for you are my strong tower, my fortress,
my refuge, when I am in distress!
17 O my strength, joyful praises I do sing!
O my stronghold, a song of joy I bring!
O my Saviour, your love for me is everything!

Psalm 60 - Does God Remember Us?
For public worship – by King David - poem of memoires for teaching - Composed When he fought Aram Naharaim and Aram Zobah, when Joab returned and struck down 12,000 Edomites in the Valley of Salt - To the tune of "Lily of the Covenant"

¹ O God! What have you abandoned us for?
You're angry with us, but please restore.
² You ripped open the land and made it shake.
Please, repair the tear, for it does quake!
³ You have shown us desperate days.
The wine you gave; made us dazed.
⁴ For those who fear you and do love,
the flag of truth, you raise above.
It brings safety from the bow,
around it now we go.
(Pause in his presence)

⁵ With your right hand help and save.
Save those who love you and praise.
God speaks, from his place of holiness.
⁶ "I divide the battle spoils, from east to west.
Shechem and Succoth, I will share.
⁷ Gilead and Manasseh are mine, I declare!
Ephraim is my helmet, producing great fighters.
Judah my sceptre, yielding kings and law writers.
⁸ Moab is my washbasin, to be my servant low.
On Edom also, my shoe I do throw,
it too will serve me so.

Over Philistia, I shout in victory!"
⁹ Who will lead me into Petra city?
Who will bring me to Edom proximity?
¹⁰ Have we really been rejected?
Will you make our armies affective?
¹¹ Please help us against the foe.
To trust in man is hollow hope.
¹² With God we gain a victory rush.
Our enemies he does trample and crush!

Psalm 61 – Protection Prayer
For public worship –
A song on stringed instruments - by King David.

¹ O God, listen to what I say.
Listen when I pray.
² Wherever I am, to you Lord, I call.
When my heart grows weak and tries to stall,
lead me to your rock, so high and tall.
³ For you have been my protection.
A refuge from enemy subjection!
⁴ I long to live in your dwelling,
to shelter in your place of hiding,
in the shadow of your outstretched wing.
Forever let it be; for all eternity.
(Pause in his presence

⁵ For you God, my vows you hear.

You've given me inheritance,
of those, your name do fear,
those that do revere.
6 You treat me like a king, with a life of expectations,
and many years, throughout the generations.
7 I will live enthroned, forever in your presence.
Guard me, with your faithful love defence!
8 Then, I will, eternally praise your name.
Day after day, I'll do the same again.
Fulfill my vow, I do proclaim!

Psalm 62 –
Faith Unshakable, Faith Unstoppable

For public worship – by King David - A melody of love's celebration – For Jeduthun.

1 Truly in God, my soul finds restoration,
for he alone is my salvation.
2 Yes, he is my salvation rock.
My Great Defender, who can't be shocked.
3 How much more can I tolerate?
They all pressure me and plan my fate!
4 They plan to topple me from my height.
In lying and cheating, they take delight.
Their mouths do bless, when they converse.
Yet, in their hearts, they all curse!
(Pause in his presence)

⁵ In my God my soul will cope,
as it finds rest and hope.
⁶ Only he is my salvation rock,
my fortress that cannot be shocked.
⁷ I depend on God, for honour and salvation.
He's my mighty rock, my sheltered destination!
⁸ Everyone, trust in him, each and every hour.
Pour out your hearts, to God, the strong tower!
(Pause in his presence)

⁹ Before God, regardless of status,
we are but a misty lie.
In comparison, they're no more,
than a breathed out sigh!
¹⁰ Don't trust in extortion,
or vainly hope in the proceeds of crime.
You may become rich,
but your heart is way out of line!
¹¹ God speaks once, but I hear it twice.
God has all power suffice!
¹² He says, "In me is all the love you need.
I reward everyone, for every deed!"

Don't trust in extortion or vainly hope in the proceeds of crime

Psalm 63 - Yearning for God

For public worship – by King David –
A song from his exile in the Wilderness of Judah.

¹ You God, are my God, I sincerely want to sync.
My whole being, thirsts and longs to link (with you)
In a dry and parched land, with nothing to drink!
In this concerning, wilderness burning,
for you my soul is yearning!
² I've seen you in your sanctuary,
from my desert territory,
and I've beheld your power and your glory.
³ Because your love is better than living,
my mouth sings glory and thanksgiving!
⁴ I will praise you for as long as I stand,
for in your name, I lift up my hands.
⁵ Like eating my favourite food, I'll be totally satisfied.
My joyful lips will sing and praise you, "Be glorified!"
⁶ Every night I lie awake and reflect,
thinking, you're like a father that never neglects.
⁷ You've helped me in everything,
⁸ so I now sing; underneath your wing!
You hold me close, now tightly I do cling!
Those who aim to kill me; will be destroyed!
⁹ The darkest depths of hell, they never will avoid.
¹⁰ The power of the sword shall be their doom.
By their own wrong doing, they'll be consumed!
¹¹ In God, the king, will dance and rejoice!
All who swear by God; make the glory choice!
As for the liars; they will lose their voice!

Psalm 64 - Destroyer of Destroyers
For public worship – A song by King David.

¹ O God, hear me, as I voice my complaint.
Protect me from my enemy constraint.
² In secret, the wicked do conspire,
as they plot and scheme their evil desire.
Please hide me from their fire!
³ Like swords, they sharpen their tongues,
then aim cruel words, like a gun.
⁴ They shoot the innocent, from ambush near.
Suddenly they shoot, without fear!
⁵ They do encourage each other, with an evil purpose.
Saying, "None will see us or ever hurt us!"
In their lair, they declare, about laying snares!
⁶ They plot unjust acts, saying,
"The perfect plan, we have devised!"
For the human mind and heart,
are cunningly organised.
All of the time, they plan the perfect crime!
⁷ But God will shoot, his unexpected blast,
as they're struck down suddenly with a gasp.
⁸ And then, their tongue, like a gun, will misfire;
destroying them and their desire.
Destroyed by their own wicked tongue,
while all the witnesses flee and run.
⁹ All people will fear and shout God's proclamation,
marvelling at his restoration and reparation!
His justice is restorative! Upright his prerogative!
¹⁰ The righteous now rejoice and hide,

with God right there, by his side.
Their hearts sing, "God is glorified!"

Psalm 65 – Creation Celebrates!
For public worship –by King David – A poetic song.

¹ O Lord God in Zion,
our silence bursts forth with praise and adoration!
Our promises to you bring fulfilment and realisation!
² You answer all prayer, not just some.
To you all people will come.
³ When we were overcome, by sinful abominations,
you forgave and cleansed our transgressions.
⁴ Blessed are the chosen, living in your courts,
your temple; the holy goodness source!
⁵ You respond, with righteous deeds of inspiration.
O God of our salvation!
You're the hope of all the nations,
and all the ocean destinations!
⁶ You are the earth-quaker, the summit-shaker,
the mountain-maker!
God of strength and power, there is none greater!
⁷ You gag the roar of the mighty oceans,
calm the waves and the worlds' commotion.
⁸ Your awesome wonders; fill the world domain,
from the rising sun, to the setting of the same,
singing, daily, joyfully, to your name!
⁹ You shower the earth with nourishment

and encouragement; through abundant, enrichment!
So you have ordained, glory bringing rain,
to give the people grain!
¹⁰ You drench the furrows and soften the clods,
softened with showers that bring forth crops.
¹¹ You bless each year with harvest provision,
overflowing carts, with more than sufficient.
¹² The wilderness grasslands overflow,
with gladness, joyous hills are clothed.
¹³ Sheep cover every meadow,
grain in the valleys below.
They shout and joy does show!
Creation celebrates!
Singing: "Praise God, who is great!"

Psalm 66 – Praise The Lord in Exaltation!
For public worship - A song of emergence.

¹ Let the whole earth sing, joy unto the King!
² Sing his glorious name, make his praise the same!
³ Say to God, "How awesome are the things you do!
Your power is great! Enemies cringe before you!
The whole earth bows to you; all day long,
forever praising your name in song!"
(Pause in his presence)

⁵ Come; see the amazing works of Gods' hand,
awesome deeds, for mankind as planned!

The things that he defined,
are bound to blow your mind!
⁶ He turned the sea into a highway.
They ran through, without delay.
On the way, they rejoiced; they were Gods' choice!
⁷ By his eternal power, he has domination,
always watching every nation.
Look out you rebels, time for realisation.
Don't rise in subordination!
No more self-exaltation!
(Pause in his presence)

⁸ Praise God, all you nations!
Hear the sound of his praise vibrations!
⁹ God holds our lives in preservation.
Keeps our feet, on his destination!
¹⁰ God tested us by cremation!
In the fiery furnace, we were tried!
Like silver and gold, we're purified!
¹¹ You've captured us, ensnared us in your net.
Then, like prisoners, placed chains around our necks.
¹² You let people trample on our heads and minds,
through fire and flood, journeyed over time.
Yet, you brought us to abundance, a place so sublime.
¹³ I come before your presence with my sacrifice.
Give all as promised; if I could, I'd do it twice.
¹⁴ The promise of my lips, muttered in distress.
Here it is! Here's my bequest!
¹⁵ I give you my best and throw it in the fire.
The sacrificial offering, I give is my heart desire!

(Pause in his presence)

16 Come and listen, all you God lovers,
I'll tell you what he's done for me and others.
17 I sobbed out loud to him, The One!
His highest praise was on my tongue
18 Yet, if I had blanked out my sin, like I didn't care,
The Lord God would have blanked out my prayer!
19 But my praise to God does rise,
for he hears and answers my cries!
20 All praise be to God, my prayer has been accepted.
His tender love for me has never been neglected!

Psalm 67 – Voices Raise, It's Time to Praise!
For public worship –
A poetic song of praise for stringed instruments.

1 May God bless us with his grace!
Look down and shine his face!
(Pause in his presence)

2 May the whole earth know your ways!
May the nations all be saved!
3 Let the people explode with praise.
God let your anthem raise!
Set the world ablaze!
4 Let the nations be glad and joyfully sing.
You're a just King, so fair and sharing,

always sheltering, forever guiding!
(Pause in his presence)

⁵ May everyone praise you and adore!
Let the people praise you more!
⁶ The earth is ripe for harvest!
God, our God, blesses us the farthest!
⁷ The blessings just keep on coming!
Then the ends of the earth shall fear him!

Psalm 68 - Victory Song
For public worship – by King David - A poetic song of praise

¹ May God arise and his enemies scattered!
Let his foes run or be battered!
² Chase them away and revoke.
Blow them like a puff of smoke!
As wax before the flame does vanish,
may the wicked before God perish!
³ With gladness let the people rejoice in your presence,
make them happy and joyful in essence!
⁴ See them sing in celebration.
See the cloud-rider in exaltation!
He is Lord of all creation!
⁵ A Father to the fatherless; the widows' defender.
That's God in his holy dwelling of splendour.
⁶ He sets the lonely, in family.
With singing, he leads the prisoners free.

To a sun-scorched land, the rebels flee!
In heartache and hostility!
⁷ Before your people, you lead the way.
Through the wilderness, you did convey.
(Pause in his presence)

⁸ The earth did tremble,
heavens opened, rain torrential.
Before God, Sinai did quake 'n' rock!
Before the God of Jacob!
⁹ O God, you gave showers in abundance.
You refreshed your weary inheritance.
¹⁰ So your people settled there
and from your bounteous care,
those in need of welfare, had their fair share.
¹¹ God Almighty declares; the Gospel word
and the mighty throng of women;
ensure that it is heard:
¹² "The kings and their armies; turn in haste and flee,
while the women at home;
share the spoils of victory!"
¹³ Even while you sleep, among the pens of sheep,
like silver I see you sparkling,
like gold I see you glistening,
underneath the doves beautiful wings.
¹⁴ When the Almighty, with one blow,
scattered the kings; what a show!
It was like Mount Zalmon, covered in snow.
¹⁵ Mount Bashan, majestic mountain,
Mount Bashan, rugged mountain,

16 Why do you and all the other mountains,
in envy look and gaze?
Staring at Mount Zion and its presence displayed.
It's where God has chosen to live his days!
17 See, the mighty chariots of God,
tens of thousands in glory.
The Lord comes, from Sinai to his sanctuary.
18 To the heavenly heights, you made ascension,
with many captives in possession.
He leads in triumphal procession.
Even the rebels, gave gifts of confession,
so they may dwell with God, in perfection.
19 Praise The Lord, the God of our salvation.
Every day he carries our burden, in consideration!
(Pause in his presence)

20 Our God is a God who saves!
From the Sovereign Lord,
comes escape from the grave!
21 God will surely crush the enemy,
shattering their strength.
He'll smash their heads in battering,
if they refuse to repent.
22 Then God says,
"In your mountain hiding place,
you can't hide from me.
I will always find you, even in the depths of the sea.
23 My people will victory declare,
crushing their enemies in despair!
Even the dogs will have their share.

They will have nothing, anywhere!"
²⁴ O God, my King,
we see your triumphant procession.
You're moving forward, into shelter and protection!
²⁵ The singers lead the way, musicians last to be seen,
young women in between, playing their tambourines.
²⁶ And they sing, "Let all God's people rejoice!
May the congregation, raise their voice.
Bless The Lord on Zion's mountain.
He's The Lord of Israel's fountain!"
²⁷ Little Benjamin; is up front leading.
There's, Judah's princes and their great throng
and along, are the princes of Zebulun
and of Naphtali; so strong!
²⁸ Lord, show us your strength and make us strong!
You've done it before, show us some more, we long.
²⁹ From your mighty temple come, don't hesitate.
Even kings will bring you gifts and donate.
³⁰ God, rebuke the deceivers,
 hiding within the congregation.
They abuse people, for their love of monetisation.
Scatter the nations, who delight, spoiling for a fight!
³¹ O God, Egyptian princes shall come.
Ethiopia will submit and succumb.
³² Sing to God, all earth's dominions.
Praise The Lord, every kingdom!
(Pause in his presence)

³³ Sing praise to he, who does ride and stride,
across the ancient, heavenly skies.

His thunderous voice splits the heavens wide!
³⁴ To the God of Israel,
for his power and majesty, proclaim!
His glory and power are in heaven's domain.
³⁵ You, God, are awesome in your glory,
in your sanctuary manifest.
The God of Israel gives power and strength,
to his people, at his behest.
May you God; be blessed!

Psalm 69 – Desperation Exclamation!

For public worship – by King David - A poetic song of praise to the tune of "Lilies"

¹ O God, save me from this strife!
The water's up to my neck and threatening my life!
² In the deep, miry swamp, I'm sinking down.
I can't stand on solid ground.
The floods over-whelm, I think I'll drown!
³ I'm exhausted in my wail, with no avail.
My throat is dry and parched; my eyes fail.
In my wait for God, I do prevail.
⁴ So many hate me without cause, too many to count.
They think that my destruction is paramount.
Do I need to restore, what is mine on account?
⁵ O God, you know my mistakes and blunders.
To you, my guilt and sin, is no wonder!
You see it all, you can recall!

⁶ Lord, God the Almighty One,
don't bring disgrace on others, for what I've done.
Keep those who live in your hope;
safe from the dishonourable slope.
O God of Israel; may those who seek,
not be shamed, because I'm weak!
⁷ For I endure such scorn for your sake,
confusion and shame has covered my face.
⁸ I am the foreigner within; I'm a stranger to my kin.
I'm an alien to my brother,
unfamiliar, an unknown other.
⁹ For you and your house, I am consumed;
by my passionate heart on fire.
I endure the insults and doom;
dumped on me by upstart liars.
¹⁰ When they see me searching and seeking,
for more of you with fasting and weeping,
they just sneer and jeer,
at my passionate pleading and believing!
¹¹ Just because I'm a humble man,
people mock me when they can.
¹² I am mocked by those who wait at the gate.
I am a song to the man in the drunken state!
¹³ O Lord, I pray, at a time of your acceptation,
in your great love, O God, grant me you salvation!
¹⁴ Rescue me, save me, from the swampy mire.
Deliver me, from the depths of trouble
and the haters desires!
¹⁵ Save me from the flood of life consumption,

or I'll go down to the pit of my destruction.
16 Answer me, Lord, in your loving, good and sweet.
In your great mercy, turn to me and greet.
17 I am your servant!
Please don't hide your face of kindness.
Come quickly! For I'm in trouble and distress!
18 Come near and rescue me! Set me free!
You can show my enemy!
19 You see my scorn, shame and disgrace.
You see my enemies, before your face.
20 My soul is crushed by scorn, my heart has been torn
And I'm left in desperation, in my broken situation.
I searched for sympathy and compassion,
it must be out of fashion.
21 When I was hungry, they fed me food so bitter.
When I was thirsty, they offered vinegar.
22 Make a trap from their banquet feast.
May their demise,
spawn from their security and peace!
23 Take away their sight, make them blind!
Forever be, feeble and trembling combined!
24 Pour out your wrath and indignation!
Burn them up, without reservation!
25 Turn their camp, into desolation!
With no one alive, in their habitation!
26 Those that you have wounded;
now face their persecution.
Their gossip about them; is a slow painful execution
27 Punish them for their constant crime.

Lock them up, till the end of time.
²⁸ From the book of life blot out their names!
Delete them, without righteous claim!
²⁹ As for me, I'm afflicted by this pain.
O God, rescue and shield me again.
³⁰ I praise and sing, in God's name.
Thanks and glory I acclaim!
³¹ This will please God, more than suffice,
greater than my gifts and sacrifice.
³² The poor and humble shall see and be relieved.
The God seekers hearts, new life received!
³³ For God, listens to those in depravity,
never despises his people in captivity.
³⁴ Praise him, all you heavens and the earth,
and the seas, moving and giving birth!
³⁵ God will save Zion and Judah;
see their reconstruction.
There his people will live in peace
and take possession.
³⁶ Inheritance, for his servants, descendants.
Those who love his name in dependence,
will live there in attendance!

**As for me, I'm afflicted
by this pain
O God, rescue and
shield me again**

Psalm 70 – Quickly Come

For public worship –
by King David - A poetic lament of un-forgetting.

¹ Come quickly Lord and set me free!
Rapidly help and restore me.
² May those who seek my death, know disillusion,
fill them with shame and confusion,
for dishonourable collusion,
turn you back on them, in exclusion!
³ May those who mock and aim, to cause me pain,
be turned back, in disgrace and shame!
⁴ May all who seek you; rejoice and celebrate!
Yearning for salvation, some do wait.
Shouting while they wait, "The Lord is great!"
⁵ As for me, I'm poor, with such great need.
Come quickly now I plead, deliver me and intercede!
Lord, come today! Please don't delay!

Psalm 71 - Song For The Golden Years

¹ In you Lord, I have taken refuge, from persecution.
Let me never be put to shame *or* confusion!
² Deliver me in your righteousness,
from those that forsake me.
Bow down your ear to me and set me free!
³ Be my rock of refuge, which I can always access.
I keep coming back to hide, when I am in distress.

You are my Rock and my Fortress!
⁴Deliver me, O God, from the hand of the iniquitous,
from the grasp of the evil and nefarious.
⁵Lord God, you're my only hopeful defence.
Since my youth, you've been my confidence.
⁶I have relied on you from birth,
from my mother's womb, you brought me forth.
I'll always praise you, for your worth!
⁷Many wonder about how I'm affected.
Yet, I know it's you, that I am protected!
⁸My mouth shall be filled with your praise,
and with your honour throughout the day.
⁹When I'm old, don't treat me like I've finished.
Don't dispose of me, when my strength has vanished.
¹⁰Behind my back, my enemies speak.
they wait to kill me, conspire and sneak,
¹¹They say, "See his God does forsake him.
Let us pursue and take him.
for no one will save him!"
¹²O God, don't be distanced!
Come quick, I need assistance!
¹³Let my accusers perish, in shame and alarm.
May scorn and disgrace, cover those who cause harm!
¹⁴As for me, I will always be, hopeful;
I will praise you more and more!
¹⁵I shall speak of your righteous demonstration,
and of your deeds of constant salvation.
Though I'm unaware of every situation!
¹⁶I'll come and proclaim your acts, so mighty!
I'll proclaim your deeds done rightly!

17 O God, you've taught me since my youth,
and I talk about, your wondrous works of truth!
18 Even when I'm old and grey,
please God, don't walk away.
Till I tell about your power in declaration,
and about your strength to the next generation.
I'll tell of your great marvels,
to those who come in expectation!
19 Your righteousness, God, reaches heavenly heights.
Nothing compares with you
and your wondrous sights!
20 Even though you've allowed us troubles and more,
many bitter and sore, my life again, you will restore.
From the depths of the earth; again, bring me forth!
21 Increase my honour and greatness.
Once again, show me comfort and wellness.
22 I praise you on the harp, God, my faithful desire.
O Holy One of Israel, I sing you praises on lyre.
23 When I sing praise to you,
my lips will shout for joy.
My Saviour delivered me, from being destroyed!
24 My tongue,
will never stop talking, about your righteous name.
As for those who seek and hunt me,
give them hurt and shame!

Psalm 72 - The Just and Righteous King
For Solomon

¹ O God, make the king a godly judge, just like you
and give the king's son, the gift of justice too.
² May he judge all people, in righteous conviction!
Bring justice to the ones with an affliction.
³ Let the mountains bring the people prosperity
and the hills bring fruit of honesty and morality.
⁴ The poor people, he'll defend
and save the children who depend.
Crush oppressors, who pretend, to be a friend!
⁵ With the sun and moons' continuation,
bring fear and adoration, through every generation!
⁶ May king Solomon, be like rain;
quenching the field's thirst,
like refreshing showers, watering the earth.
⁷ In his days, may the righteous increase
and prosper until the moon does cease.
⁸ From sea to sea, may he rule and reign,
from the river to the end of the terrain.
⁹ Before him, may nomad tribes bow
and his enemies, bite dust now!
¹⁰ From every distant king, come gifts and offerings.
From countries far, let them tributes bring.
¹¹ May all kings, fall at his feet
and every nation serve his seat.
¹² For when they plead, he saves those in need.
He will aid the poor and those with help no more.
¹³ He takes pity on those too weak to survive.

He'll keep them alive and help them thrive!
14 He'll rescue them from violence and oppression,
for their bloodline is precious, in his vision.
15 Long live the king!
Worldly wealth, let people bring,
may their prayer and praises sing.
A constant source of blessing!
16 Throughout the land, grant an abundant harvest.
On the hilltops, let it be the best.
Like Lebanon, let us be blessed!
17 May his name endure, to the end of time;
may it continue as the sunshine!
Through him, the nations will be blessed,
then everyone will bless the rest!
18 Praise be; to The Lord God, God of the Israel nation!
The God of deeds and wonders, beyond expectation!
19 Forever praise his glorious name!
Fill the earth with his glory! Amen, again and again!
20 This concludes the poem sung,
      by David, Jesse's son.

Throughout the land grant an abundant harvest. On the hilltops let it be the best

Collection Three
Psalms of
Worship and God's House

Psalm 73 - God's Poetic Justice
A psalm of Asaph

¹ God is good to Israel; no one can deny,
to the pure, with a heartfelt cry.
² Yet, my story was almost different,
nearly missed all the significance.
³ For I envied those who are arrogant,
when I saw prosperity in the wicked and malevolent.
⁴ They have no struggles; despite their wrongs.
They have no scuffles; though their bodies are strong.
⁵ Everyday burdens, they don't have any.
Good health, they have plenty.
⁶ They flaunt their pride and opulence,
with lives of cruelty and violence!
⁷ Their bitter hearts have sin within it.
Their evil imaginations have no limit.
⁸ They scoff, speaking with malice and aggression;
with such arrogance, threaten with oppression.
The loudmouths don't fear God!
⁹ They swagger through the earth,
with their blaspheming gob!
Cursing where they trod, bragging roughshod!
¹⁰ Yet the people keep coming back,

to listen to more of their claptrap.
11 They say, "How does God know what we do?
He really doesn't have a clue?"
12 These are the wicked ones, oh my!
They never have to try, sit back while riches multiply.
13 Have I been a fool, to play by all the rules?
Is pure innocence in vain? Do I give into the strain?
14 Every day I feel affliction,
morning punishments and conviction!
15 If I had succumbed in the painful situation
and spoken in frustration,
I would have betrayed the next generation.
16 When this, I tried to comprehend,
it was too much pain, though I did intend.
17 When, in the end;
I entered God's sanctuary and protection.
Then I understood their destiny is rejection!
18 They're on the slippery road, to destruction,
facing fear, dread and abruption!
19 Instantly their good life will be gone,
swept away in terror, to the place that they belong!
They thought that they could rule,
they're nothing more than fools.
20 They disappear like a dream when one awakes.
You despise them and their pretentious mistakes!
21 At this sight, I did grieve,
truth filled my heart and I believed.
22 I was so flippant! Senseless and ignorant!
Lord, I'm a brute-beast before you, in a predicament!
23 Yet, with you, I do stand,

you hold me by my right hand.
²⁴ You're my counsellor, guiding, writing my story,
afterwards, you will take me into glory!
²⁵ Lord, you're all that I need, in the heavenly height.
Beside you, earth has no desire
or gives me no delight.
²⁶ Lord, in my own strength I may fail,
but when I trust in your heart strength,
forever I prevail!
²⁷ Those that are far from you; will one day perish.
You will destroy the unfaithful,
you hate them and never cherish!
But as for me; near God, is where I need to be.
²⁸ In God I put my trust, for The Lord is my protection.
Tell the world I must;
of your deeds of such perfection!

Psalm 74 – Your Restoration, For Devastation

A poem of instruction – by Asaph

¹ O God, why do you always treat us like rejects?
We are your people, your loyal subjects.
Please stop your smouldering anger in detest!
² Don't forget! We're your chosen nation,
purchased way back in liberation,
freedom; emancipation.
The tribe of your inheritance, the redeemed!

Remember your residence,
Mount Zion, it's your scene.
³ Turn toward this perpetual devastation.
The enemy brought desecration,
to your place of protection.
See the ruins and desolation!
⁴ Your enemy entered your Holy Place,
with a roaring cry.
Setting up banners and idols, to deny and defy.
⁵ They behaved like a logging crew,
wielding axes, cutting through!
Blasting through thicket wood,
like they own the neighbourhood.
⁶ The carved wooden panels were all smashed,
as the axes and hatchets, bashed and crashed!
⁷ They burned your sanctuary to the ground,
for evil gain,
violating the dwelling place of your holy name.
⁸ Then they boasted,
"Let's totally smash them down!"
They set fire to all of God's worship places,
burnt them to the ground!"
⁹ We see no signs and miracles,
no prophets left to make the call.
No one knows how long, we all, will endure.
¹⁰ God, how long will the enemy mock and jeer?
Will the foe revile your name, year after year?
¹¹ Hidden your hand remains,
your right hand is restrained.

Take it out and destroy them in pain!
¹² But God is my King, from years of participation,
I know his reputation. He gives the earth salvation!
¹³ You split open the sea, by your power,
smashed Egypt's head, as the water devoured.
¹⁴ You crushed the monster's head and its features
and fed the remains to the desert creatures.
¹⁵ You brought forth fountains, from the rock.
The mighty flowing rivers, you did block.
¹⁶ Yours is the day and the night.
You established sun and moon, in your sight.
¹⁷ You formed the earth's boundaries, for a reason.
You created summer; winter, all four seasons.
¹⁸ God, don't forget how the enemy mock and shame,
how the foolish people revile your name.
¹⁹ Don't sacrifice your dove to the wild beast.
Always remember your people with the least.
²⁰ Remember you made us a promise,
for darkness covers the province.
It's a hiding place for the violent and dishonest.
²¹ Do not let the oppressed retreat in shame;
may the poor and needy praise your name!
²² Rise up, O God, and defend your lot;
remember how fools continually mock.
²³ Don't ignore the clamouring enemy cries;
continuous enemy roaring cries,
against you does rise!
It's time to stand against, time for defence!

Psalm 75 - A Cup of Judgement and Fury

For public worship – by Asaph - A poetic song –
To the tune of "Do Not Destroy"

¹ We praise you, God,
we praise you, for your Name is close;
of your wonderful deeds, you must boast!
² Then God says, "I do choose the time allocation.
I judge in fair and just arbitration.
³ When the earth and people start to quake;
I hold its pillars firm, make no mistake!"
(Pause in his presence)

Then God gives the proud a roasting,
"Stop your arrogant boasting!"
⁴ To those full of iniquity,
"Don't think you will ever resist me!
⁵ Why do you speak such arrogant pride?
Don't come against me and my side!"
⁶ I know this much, wherever you originate,
the things we do, don't make us great!
⁷ It's God who is our Judge.
He lifts one up for what he does,
to another he does bear a grudge!
⁸ See God's foaming judgement cup,
fury within, he filled it up!
Filled up for those with sin,
so they will drink it in.
Drink, don't stop! Drink every drop!
⁹ To Jacob's God, I always praise,

declaring joy, all my days!
¹⁰ Then this is what God says,
"I'll smash the power of evil, I'll make it halt!
As for the righteous, I give power and exalt!"

Psalm 76 – Awesome God
For public worship – by Asaph –
A poetic song on stringed instruments

¹ In Judah, God is well notorious.
In Israel, his name is great and glorious.
² He makes Jerusalem his residence.
Mount Zion is his dwelling presence.
³ There he broke the flashing arrows that soar,
smashed shields and swords, weapons of war.
(Pause in his presence)

⁴ Lord, you shine with radiance,
more majestic than your mountain abundance!
⁵ In your presence, mighty men are stunned,
where they stand.
Not one paralysed warrior could raise a hand!
⁶ When Jacob's God, roared his rebuking cry;
then, both man and horse, collapsed and died!
⁷ You alone are to be feared, in reverence.
For when you are angry,
who can stand in your presence?
⁸ From heaven you announced your sentence.

The earth feared, in still silence.
⁹ You arise to punish, wickedness suppressed.
On the earth, you save the meek and oppressed.
(Pause in his presence)

¹⁰ Your wrath and power demonstration,
brings mankind's transformation.
All earth's population,
will now praise your name.
The wrath survivors are restrained!
¹¹ If you promise to God,
your fulfilment must be clear.
Let everyone that's near,
bring gifts to the One to be feared!
¹² See earth's ruler's, spirits squashed like a worm.
The ungodly kings, do fear and squirm!

Psalm 77 – God Where Are You?
For public worship – by Asaph – For Jeduthun.

¹ I cried to God to help my need.
I cried to God, please listen with heed!
² I sought The Lord, in my despair.
Each night, I raise my hands in prayer.
I ignore all comfort and care.
³ God, as I remember you, I groan in my complaint.
As I meditate, my spirit grows faint.
(Pause in his presence)

⁴ I don't have a wink of sleep,
too troubled to pray and speak!
⁵ I think about how things used to be,
the long gone years, of prosperity.
⁶ Then,
I recall my night-time worship songs, in the past.
My heart meditated and my spirit did ask:
⁷ "Will The Lord always, reject and neglect?
Where's you favour? Will you direct?
⁸ Has your unfailing love vanished, forever gone?
Will your promises fail for all time long?
⁹ Where is your love? Have you forgotten?
Is it out of fashion?
Are you so angry, you're out of compassion?"
(Pause in his presence)

¹⁰ Then I cried; "Lord, the problem, I have identified.
It's totally my fault; you're not by my side,
that I no longer see your right hand provide.
¹¹ O Lord, your great deeds, I'll never deny.
I remember your miracles, in days gone by.
¹² To your works, I show consideration,
to your awesome wonders, my meditation."
¹³ Your ways God, are holy and true.
There is no other god, compares to you!
¹⁴ You are God of miraculous demonstration.
You show your power, among the nations.
¹⁵ With your mighty arm, you did rescue.
The sons of Jacob and Joseph, say it's true!
You brought them through!

(Pause in his presence)

16 The Red Sea and the Jordan; saw you and did fear.
The deep oceans shuddered, when they saw you near!
17 Storm clouds opened and a deluge poured.
The thunder clapped, with a mighty roar.
Lightning flashed forth, in forks!
18 Your boom bellowed in the whirlwind,
the world, by lightning illumined!
The whole earth in fear; trembled as you came near.
19 Through the mighty seas, you formed a highway.
You left no footprints on display.
Not a single trace, of your presence in that place.
20 Like Moses and Aaron, led the gathered herd,
your loving hand, led the people forward.

Psalm 78 – Reflection Instruction
Asaph's reflective poetic song.

1 My people; hear now my revelation.
Listen to my words of instruction,
receive with reflection.
2 With a parable, I will speak,
uttering words ancient and antique.
3 Stories we have heard and known,
things that our ancestors have shown.
It was all told, in days of old.
4 We'll not hide them, from their procreation,

we'll share them with the next generation.
The praiseworthy deeds of The Lord, affirmed.
His might and wonders, he has performed.
⁵ In Jacob and Israel, he set decrees and laws,
told our ancestors to teach the children, to be in awe.
⁶ May they be known to the next generation,
and their children's children, in perpetuation.
⁷ Then in God, they place their hope,
remember his deeds to cope.
Then they understand,
the need to keep his commands.
⁸ That they wouldn't be as their ancestors,
stubborn and rebellious.
Their hearts for God were loyal-less,
spirits faithless and contentious
⁹ Like the men of Ephraim,
armed with bow and spear.
Then when the battle came near,
they ran away in fear.
¹⁰ They didn't keep God's promises,
refused to live by his policies.
¹¹ Their memories didn't last,
forgot his wonders from the past.
¹² Even the Egypt exodus flight,
the epic miracle of his might.
They forgot the delivery of Jehovah
and his power at the passing over.
¹³ He divided the sea and led them all;
made water stand up like a wall!
¹⁴ A pillar of cloud, led the way in the light;

a pillar of fire stood guard at night.
15 He split desert rocks, with springs to please,
with more water than abundant seas.
16 Streams poured forth from rock;
flowing rivers that did shock!
17 Yet, against him, they continued to sin,
in rebelliousness,
against the Most High God in the wilderness.
18 In their hearts, they put God to the test,
demanding food they craved and obsessed.
19 Against God; they did confess,
"Can God really spread a table in the wilderness?
20 Yes, true, he struck a rock and water gushed out,
but where's the bread and meat?
We really do doubt!"
21 When God heard their moaning,
his fury was incensed.
His anger towards his people became so intense!
22 For they didn't trust, instead they feared.
They doubted his deliverance and that he is near.
23 Yet, he gave a command to the skies above
and opened the heavenly doors of love.
24 Manna rained down for the people to eat,
the grain of grace, fell such a treat.
25 Angel food appeared, at God's will
and all of the people had their fill!
26–27 The heavenly winds, he made them blow,
then provided meat and foul, for all below.
They ate all, with more to show.
28 He made food come down, in their sight,

all around their tents, was such delight!
²⁹ They ate till they were more than stuffed,
he had given them what they craved and did lust.
³⁰ Then before they turned from their crave pursued,
even while food was still being chewed,
³¹ God's anger and wrath rose against them.
He killed the strongest, of Israel's men!
³² In spite of all this, their sinning didn't leave;
despite the sight of wonders, they didn't believe.
³³ He cut short their futile lives, in disaster,
with nothing to show but fear, thereafter.
³⁴ When he cared, they thought it inane,
whenever God killed them in pain,
they came, quickly running back again.
³⁵ They remembered that God was their Rock,
in times of trouble,
that God Most High,
redeemed them from the struggle.
³⁶ They spoke flattery and deceit,
a bunch of lying cheats!
³⁷ Their hearts had turned away;
insincere and disgraceful.
Your promises disobeyed; no longer true and faithful!
³⁸ Yet, he mercifully forgave their sin and corruption,
saving them over and over from destruction.
He restrained his wrath and anger eruption.
³⁹ He remembered that they were mere flesh and bone.
Here today, but tomorrow they're gone.
⁴⁰ In the wilderness,

they were rebellious, full of bitterness.
In the wasteland; they grieved him and slammed!
41 Repeatedly they ignored God, testing and stoking,
the Holy One of Israel, incensing and provoking!
42 They forgot his mighty power;
the enemies that devour
and their redemption hour.
43 They forgot the Egyptian plagues,
of wrath and thunder,
disregarded the epic signs and wonders.
44 He filled their rivers with blood pollution,
with nothing to drink, such persecution.
45 His next surprise, the venomous flies,
devouring them from the inside.
Then frogs came to destroy the lot.
46 Grasshopper and locust; ate their crop.
47 A deluge of hail and a touch of frost,
turned all the fruit trees, to stinking compost.
48 The lightning and frozen rain,
caused all their cattle to be slain,
with more pain on top of pain.
49 Finally, they experienced the full wrath of God,
as he unleashed his angelic killing squad!
Such anger, distress and indignation!
He sent sorrow and devastation!
50-51 He prepared a path for his anger and scorn.
No escape from death, the Egyptians did mourn.
He killed their beasts and their first born!
They should have heeded when warned!
52 Then,

he brought his people out like a flock in despair;
he led them like sheep, through the wilderness,
with a shepherd care.
53 They were afraid,
but he led them safely on dry ground,
but their enemies he led into the sea,
where they all drowned!
54 He brought them to the border, of his Holy Land,
to the hill country, taken by his right hand.
55 He went before, driving out the nations,
then divided their land, a legacy allocation,
so Israel's tribes, could dwell in their habitation.
56 Yet, they tempted God,
with rebelling and provoking.
They turned away, from God Most High,
as if they were joking.
57 They were disloyal and faithless,
like their ancestors all the same.
Twisted, like a warped and deceitful bow,
impossible to aim.
58 With their high places, they angered him,
their idols aroused his jealousy within!
59 When God heard them,
he was angry with their lack of trust,
so he rejected Israel with disgust.
60 From his dwelling place at Shiloh,
he did walk away,
abandoning where he had lived with them each day.
61 He sent the ark of his might into captivity,
his splendour into the hands of the enemy.

⁶² In battle, their enemies were victorious,
for God was angry and so furious.
He turned his back, they took the flack;
with swords they were hacked!
⁶³ Their young men were consumed by fire.
The young women faced a situation dire.
Never to hear their wedding song,
with all of the young men gone!
⁶⁴ Their priests were all killed, dead!
The widows had no time for a tear to be shed,
before they too bled!
⁶⁵ Then The Lord awoke as if he'd slept some time,
as a warrior wakes from the stupor of wine.
⁶⁶ He beat back his enemies again;
inflicting them to constant shame.
⁶⁷ Then he rejected Joseph's tribe,
where the Covenant Ark, did reside.
⁶⁸ Instead, he chose the tribe of Judah,
over and above,
and Mount Zion, which he did love.
⁶⁹ He established there, his temple height,
strong as the earth, forever in his sight.
⁷⁰ He chose David, his servant,
a shepherd, caring and observant.
⁷¹ From protecting sheep, in their defence,
to protecting Israel, his inheritance
⁷² So, David was the shepherd, with an upright heart.
He skilfully led them, doing his part.

Psalm 79
Disaster is Here, We Need You Near
Asaph's poetic song

¹ O God, your nation's legacy has been invaded.
Your holy temple; violated and raided.
Jerusalem has been defiled and degraded!
² They left your servant's bodies, where they did die,
rotting food, for beasts and the birds of the sky.
³ Your servant's blood, poured out in flood.
The city is in dread; with no one to bury the dead.
⁴ We face humiliation and contempt,
from neighbours who surround us;
a mocking and derision, from those all around us.
⁵ O Lord, will your anger ever expire?
Will your jealousy burn like a raging fire?
⁶ Pour out your wrath on the ignorant nations,
for they show you no love affirmation.
Ignorant they remain, and do not call your name!
⁷ They attacked us, devouring the land,
leaving it desolate and damned.
⁸ Do not hold against us the sins of past generations;
may your mercy come quick
to meet us in desperation.
⁹ Help us, Saviour God,
for the glory and sake of your name.
Forgive us and deliver us, from our pain,
again and again!
¹⁰ Why should the nations mock us, saying,
"Where is this God of yours?"

Let vengeance be yours, for the suffering we endured!
¹¹ Hear now the prisoners, as they groan and sigh.
With your strong arm,
preserve those condemned to die!
¹² Lord,
for all the insults aimed at you and negative exposure,
pay it back, to the mockers and scoffers,
seven times over!
¹³ Then we the holy nation,
give thanks and affirmation.
We're in it for the duration!
Sing praise and proclamation,
from generation to generation!

Psalm 80 – Salvation Restoration

For public worship - Asaph's poetic song –
To the tune of "Lilies of the Covenant"

¹ Listen, shepherd of Israel, we know Joseph's story.
Ride between cherubim, shine forth in glory!
Joseph's flock you did lead; listen to me plead!
² With Ephraim, Benjamin and Manasseh,
in your sight,
come and save us , awaken your great might.
³ Make your face shine upon us,
Almighty God, give us restoration,
show your commendation, give us your salvation.
⁴ O Lord God Almighty, who is fair and does care,

how long will you be angry,
with your people's prayer?
⁵ You fed us sorrow, grief and fear,
made us drink buckets full of tears.
⁶ To our neighbours, we are like a thorn (in their side),
but now they just mock and scorn, in their pride.
⁷ Come back, O God, of the angelic squad,
shine your face, give us restoration,
show your appreciation, give us your salvation!
⁸ Like a young vine from Egypt,
we were your transplantation.
You planted us in the land,
having chased off all the nations.
⁹ You cleared the ground for it, as planned;
then it grew deep roots, filling the land.
¹⁰ Its shade covered the mountain side,
its bough like cedars broad and wide.
The vineyard was abundant; mighty and resplendent.
¹¹ Its branches reached down to the coast;
and shoots, as far as the river to boast.
¹² Why have you broken the walls in dispute?
Now trespassers come and steal the fruit!
¹³ Wild beasts breakthrough all the defections;
leaving us without protection.
All the wildlife feed, taking what they need.
¹⁴ Come back, O God, of the angelic squad.
Look down from heaven and see our pain.
Come down and care for this vine again!
¹⁵ Protect the root, shoot and fruit;
that your right-hand planted in vain.

The one that you love, raise up the one,
for yourself, raise up the son!
¹⁶ Enemies cut down our vine and burned it in the fire,
may they perish at your rebuke, may death transpire.
¹⁷ Let your hand rest on the man,
the one sat at your right hand,
You raised him for yourself, the son of man.
¹⁸ Then we will not depart from you again.
Revive us, and we will call, on your name.
¹⁹ O, Almighty God, of the angelic squad,
shine your face, give us restoration,
show your affirmation, give us your salvation!

Psalm 81 – Celebration for Provision

For public worship - Asaph's poetic song set to Philistine Lute, with the melody of "For the Feast of Harvest"

¹ To God our strength, we sing and regale.
Shout for joy, to the God of Israel!
² Start the music, beat the drum,
the sweet harp and lyre, has already begun.
³ When the moon is full, blow the trumpet call!
Blow it for the new moon, the day of festival.
⁴ For God, gave us seasons of jubilation,
for us to rejoice in celebration.
The God of Jacob, decreed with authorisation!
⁵ Against Egypt, God went out!
He gave us these feasts, to remind us about.

Then I heard a strange voice shout:
6 "From their breaking backs, I removed the weight,
from your toil and strife, I did liberate.
7 You called in distress and I came to rescue,
from a thundercloud, I answered you.
At the waters of Meribah, I tested too."
(Pause in his presence)

8 "I warn you, my people, but do you hear?
It's time Israel, that you opened your ears!
9 I'm the only God; that you should have,
worship just me and you'll be glad.
10 I, The Lord your God, freed you from captivity.
I'll fill your mouth with a decree,
then you will see! So shall it be!
11 But my people just ignored my voice.
Israel rebelled, they made their choice.
12 I gave them up to their stubborn hearts,
then left them, as I did depart!
13 If my people would only listen one day.
If Israel, would only follow my way!
14 Then, I would defeat your every foe
and tell each one of them to go!
15 Those who hate The Lord; will cringe and cower,
they will suffer punishment, every eternal hour.
16 But you would be fed with the finest of wheat,
with honey from the rock, as a satisfying treat."

Psalm 82 – The Moment of Truth

Asaph's poetic song

¹ All stand! This court is in session!
God, judges the gods and hears their confession!
² Saying,
"How long will you judges defend the unjust?
Why show favour, to the wicked without trust?"
(Pause in his presence)

³ "Defend the weak and the fatherless;
fight for the poor and the oppressed.
⁴ Rescue the weak and the powerless;
deliver from the grip of wicked sourness.
⁵ Those gods that profess; are in ignorance darkness,
while the justice system foundations stress,
shaking in duress!
⁶ I said,
'You're gods, since you judge with power I give.
You're sons of the Most High, my representatives!'
⁷ Yet, you will die, like any other human being.
You'll be buried in the ground,
like every ruler there has been.
Yes, you will be a 'has-been'!"
All stand!
God, THE Judge is in command!
⁸ O God, judge the earth, as you do,
for all the nations, belong to you!

Psalm 83 - God, Speak Out, Time to Shout!
Asaph's poetic song

^{1} O God, speak out! It's time to shout!
Listen without a doubt!
Sound the klaxon! It's time for action!
^{2} See how your enemies roar and growl,
how your foes lift up their heads and howl!
^{3} Against your people, they cunningly conspire,
plot against those you cherish and admire.
^{4} They say, "Come now, let's end this nation's story,
we'll delete the name, 'Israel' from history!
Let us enjoy, as we destroy!"
^{5} See, they plot together as one.
Against you, they are allied scum!
^{6} You see the sons; of Edom and the Ishmaelites,
of Moab and the Hagrites,
^{7} Byblos, Ammon and Amalek,
they're all ready to wreck.
^{8} The people of Tyre and Philistia,
join Lot's lot, from Assyria.
The whole pack, poised to attack!
(Pause in his presence)

^{9} Do as you did to the Midianites,
defeated by Gideon, in your might,
as to Sisera and Jabin, in Kishon's sight.
^{10} Show us a battle of Endor repeat, crushed in defeat!
Rotting corpses, piled high, like a stinking dung heap.
^{11} You brought them pain, now do it again!

Make their nobles die, like Oreb and Zeeb,
their princes like Zebah and Zalmunna,
make them bleed!
¹² For they said, "Let's grab God's land,
out from his hand!"
¹³ Blow them with your little puff,
like the wind blowing dust!
¹⁴ As the forest fire does consume
and a single flame a mountain doomed.
So burn them, scorch them, torch them, boom!
¹⁵ Chase them, with your tempest again;
terrify them with your hurricane.
¹⁶ O Lord, cover their faces with shame,
so they seek, the glory of your name.
¹⁷ May they always feel guilty, with dismal frustration;
let them perish in disgrace and humiliation.
¹⁸ Let them know that your name is, Lord of all worth,
that you, Most High God, are exalted over the earth!

Psalm 84 - Desiring God

For public worship – By the Sons of Korah –
Set to Philistine lute.

¹ See your dwelling place, so bright;
O Lord God, with great might!
² O Lord, my soul deeply longs to be in your court.
Living God, my heart and flesh cry for support!
³ Even the birds have built a nest,

where their eggs can be caressed.
Your alters they're among,
where they will raise their young.
My King and God, Lord of the angelic squad,
those who live in your house are blessed.
Always in your presence, they worship and rest!
(Pause in his presence)

[5] Blessed are those, whose strength is in your embrace,
their hearts are a highway to your holy place!
[6] They journey through the dark valley of tears,
where pleasant springs do appear.
The early rain drops are a blessing to hear.
[7] They grow stronger and stronger, each year.
Then, before God in Zion, each will appear.
[8] Hear my cry, O God of the angelic squad!
Listen to my heartfelt prayer, O Israel's God.
(Pause in his presence)

[9] O God, you alone, are our shield,
see your anointed ones, with favour revealed.
[10] Better is one day in your courts,
than a thousand elsewhere.
In God's house, I'd mind the door,
rather than live in the wicked glare.
[11] For The Lord, is a ray of sunshine;
protecting us like a life saver.
He gives us, glory, grace and favour.
Those who live a life of integrity;
will lack nothing for posterity!

¹² O Lord God, of the angelic squad, so true,
blessed is the one who trusts in you!

Psalm 85 - Merciful Restoration
For public worship - A prophetic song –
by the Sons of Korah.

¹ Lord, you showed your land favourable reward.
The captives of Jacob; have been restored!
As your love has been poured!
² You forgave all of our wickedness
and cover all our sinfulness.
(Pause in his presence)

³ You set your wrath aside; your anger you denied.
⁴ God of salvation, send your restoration;
hide your indignation.
⁵ Will you always bare a grudge?
Will your anger never budge?
⁶ Will you revive this generation?
Will we rejoice in celebration?
⁷ Time for your love revelation!
Grant us your mercy salvation!
⁸ Lord God, I will listen to what you say.
He promises peace for all who faithfully pray,
but don't let them turn to foolish ways.
⁹ Surely, his salvation is near, to those who do fear?
That his glory may dwell, on hilltop and dell!

¹⁰ Mercy and truth become one in bliss;
Righteousness and peace join with a kiss.
¹¹ Faithfulness springs up from the ground;
righteousness, from heaven shines down.
¹² Goodness comes from God's indulgence;
as the land yields a harvest of abundance!
¹³ Righteousness goes on ahead;
it makes a path, for his feet to tread!

Psalm 86 - A Prayer of Belief
A prayer of King David

¹ Hear me, Lord, and answer me,
for I am poor and needy.
² Guard my life, I'm a faithful friend,
save your servant, I trust and depend.
My God, come now descend!
³ Your mercy Lord, please send!
I call all day, from start to end!
⁴ Make me your servant to rejoice.
God, it's you I trust, you are my choice!
⁵ Lord, your loving and forgiveness does astound.
To all who call,
your over-flowing mercy does abound!
⁶ Lord hear my cry and please reply.
Don't deny mercy when I cry!
⁷ I call your name, when I am in distress.
I know that you answer and never suppress!

⁸ Lord, there's no other god like you.
You are the greatest, just look what you do!
You're one of a kind, so rare;
no other we find to compare!
⁹ Come and worship, all you nations.
Lord, before you, bring glorification!
¹⁰ You are so great, working wonders for mankind.
God, you are unique, matchless, one of a kind!
¹¹ Lord, teach me your way; fan my faith into flame.
Direct my heart, that I may; in awe fear your name.
¹² Lord God, with my whole heart, I give you praise!
I will glorify your name, always, all my days!
¹³ You show me love and mercy,
with tons of affection.
You delivered me from the depths
of death and affliction.
¹⁴ O God, the arrogant attack me with such strife,
this ruthless rabble, plan to take my life.
As for you, they neglect; before you, no respect!
¹⁵ Lord God, you ooze compassion and grace,
slow to anger, abounding in love and faith embrace!
¹⁶ Turn to me, have mercy and be gracious,
grant this servant strength outrageous.
I serve you, as did my mum;
I serve you, my number One!
¹⁷ Show me a sign; that your goodness does remain,
when the haters see it, they'll be full of shame.
You give me your support, regardless of my faults.

Psalm 87 – The Spring of Life and Joy
A prophetic song – by the Sons of Korah

¹ Jerusalem and the Temple, the place that God built;
stands on the holy hills.
² More than any other place,
The Lord loves Zion's gates.
As for Israel's other dwelling places, they under-rate.
³ Zion is absolute glorification!
The city of God, made proclamation!
(Pause in his presence)

⁴ God says, "Egypt and Ethiopia;
Iraq, Tyre and Philistia.
You acknowledge me, I do see.
You boast, you were born in Zion city."
⁵ Yes, of Zion, it will be said on earth,
"This man and that man; there had birth,
for the Most High God, will establish her worth."
⁶ He registers their names, counting them dear.
By their names he writes, "This one born here!"
(Pause in his presence)

⁷ They will make music and joyfully sing.
"Your life within me, does spring!"

Psalm 88
May Your Intent, Save My Torment!
For public worship - A Reflective Poem –
by the Sons of Korah.
To the tune of "Pierced", by Heman the Ezrahite.

¹ Lord God, Yahweh, come to my rescue.
Night and day, I cry out to you!
² May my prayer, be with you nigh.
Don't deny! Listen when I cry!
³ My life is full of trouble.
Death draws near, in my struggle!
⁴ They've all left me here to die,
like a man without strength to even try.
⁵ I'm abandoned with the dead,
in their graves they lay slain.
You forget the things I said,
no more your care remains.
⁶ You've thrown me in the pit of neglect,
down in the lowest, darkest, depths!
⁷ Heavy, upon me; lies your rage,
I'm drowning in your sorrowful waves
(Pause in his presence)

⁸ From me, you snatched my dearest friends,
making me, repulsive to them.
I'm trapped, no sign of the end!
⁹ My weary eyes are filled with sorrow.
Lord I call you, like there's no tomorrow.
To you I spread my hands, and hope you understand.

10 Will you show wonders to the diseased?
Do their spirits praise you, when released?
(Pause in his presence)

11 Is your love declared in the tomb?
Is faithfulness preached, in the doom?
12 Are your wonders known in the darkness,
and your righteousness, in the place of forgetfulness?
13 Lord, to you I cry and pray,
at the dawn of each new day.
Hear what I have to say!
14 O Lord, why do you turn me away?
Why hide from me, every day?
15 My whole life, I've feared death's stare!
I have carried your terrors, I'm in despair!
16 Your fierce anger has knocked me flying.
Your horrors destroyed me, no denying!
17 24/7, like a flood they surround.
I feel so swamped, I think I'll drown!
18 You took my friends and neighbours, I feel bereft!
Darkness is the closest friend; that I now have left!

Psalm 89 - Will You Ever Accept Us?
Reflective Poems by Ethan the Ezrahite

Poem One – God's Promises to David
[1] I will sing of The Lord's great love,
for the eternal duration.
With my mouth, I shout out,
your faithfulness, from generation to generation!
[2] "Your love always stands firm!"
That's my declaration.
Your faithfulness in heaven; has a firm foundation!
[3] You said, "I've made a promise, to the one I chose,
my servant David, I swear he knows.
[4] I'll establish your line, for the eternal duration.
I'll build up your throne, for all generations."
(Pause in his presence)

[5] O Lord, let heaven praise the wonders that you do.
Let the angels praise, your faithfulness too.
[6] For who, in the skies above,
can compare with The Lord all seeing?
Who is like The Lord, among the heavenly beings?
[7] In the angelic council, God is greatly feared.
He's more awesome, than all who stand near!
Not one is like you! Lord God,
commander of the angelic squad.
[8] Lord, your might knows no bounds!
All around you, faithfulness shines and surrounds!
[9] You rule the surging sea of harm;
when the waves rise up, you make them calm.

¹⁰ You crushed Egypt, one of the slain.
Your strong arm scattered enemies again.
¹¹ The heavens are yours and the earth is too.
You're the Creator and all belongs to you.
¹² The north and south, you created the same.
The mighty mountains, still praise your name.
¹³ Your mighty arm, proves a powerful demonstration.
Your strong right arm raised, in exaltation!
¹⁴ The foundation,
of your throne, is justice and righteousness.
Going before you is, love and faithfulness.
¹⁵ Blessed are those who have appreciation,
they rejoice in acclamation.
Lord, they walk in the light, of your manifestation.
¹⁶ In your name they rejoice all day.
In your righteousness they do celebrate.
¹⁷ Glory and strength, is from you our source.
Your favour makes us stronger, by recourse!
¹⁸ Our shield belongs to The Lord, who never fails,
our king to the Holy One of Israel.

Poem Two – God Always Keeps His Promises
Through prophetic visitation,
you spoke to your faithful nation,
making this proclamation,
¹⁹⁻²⁰ "On a warrior, I bestow strength and affirmation.
I raise this young man, David, in exaltation.
With oil, he's anointed for my nation.
²¹ My hand will him sustain,

my arm will make his strength remain.
²² The enemy will not get the better of him;
the wicked will not oppress and win.
²³ Before his face, I'll crush his foe;
smash the haters, with a blow!
²⁴ My faithful love for him will not be halted.
Through my name, his strength will be exalted.
²⁵ Over the sea, I give him jurisdiction.
Over the rivers, his right hand has domination!
²⁶ He will cry out to me, in affirmation,
"You're my Father, my God; the Rock of Salvation!"
²⁷ I will appoint him to be my firstborn son,
the most exalted of kings, over everyone!
²⁸ My love for him; will always prevail.
I'll never break my promise, I'll never fail.
²⁹ His off-spring will last forever more.
His throne as long as the heavens, will endure.
³⁰ If his sons ignore,
my law,
and fail to follow my instruction,
³¹ if they violate my decrees, failing my direction,
³² I will punish their transgression,
with the rod of pain correction.
³³ But my love will never fail (him).
My faithfulness will prevail, without betrayal.
³⁴ My promise with David, I will not revoke.
No word I said; will ever be broke.
³⁵ For I swore, by my holiness, I cannot defy.
To David, I will never lie!
³⁶ His kin will continue, forever more.

His throne will endure.
37 Like the moon, it'll always be recognised,
a faithful witness in the skies."
(Pause in his presence)

Poem Three – Why Has David Been Defeated?
[38] Yet, you've rejected and spurned!
What have you done?
Angry you've become, with your anointed one!
[39] From your promise with your servant,
you have backed down.
You stripped away his crown,
thrown it to the ground.
[40] You tore down his walls of defence,
destroyed his stronghold, so immense!
[41] All that pass him by; now steal and profiteer,
while his neighbours, mock and jeer!
[42] You chose the side of his enemy,
watch them rejoice in victory!
[43] You turned back his sword edge, in dismay.
In the battle, you have turned away.
[44] You put down, his splendorous crown.
You've thrown his throne; down to the ground.
[45] The days of his youth, no more remain.
He is covered, with a shroud of shame!
(Pause in his presence)

Poem Four – God, Rescue Us!

⁴⁶ Will you always hide from me? Is this your desire?
How long will your anger burn like raging fire?
⁴⁷ Remember, how short is my life of fragility?
For what futility, have you created humanity!
⁴⁸ Who can live and from death be saved?
Who can escape the power of the grave?
(Pause in his presence)

⁴⁹ Lord, where is your former love and kindness?
You promised David your faithfulness?
⁵⁰ Don't forget Lord,
how your servant has been mocked in accusation.
Lord,
it seems my heart is carrying,
the pain of all the nations.
⁵¹ Remember, the hater's insults and persecution,
piled upon your anointed one.
⁵² However, forever Lord, our praises we bestow.
Amen! So be it! Make it so!

You tore down his walls of defence destroyed his stronghold so immense!

Collection Four
Psalms of Our Journey on Earth

Psalm 90 – The Everlasting God!
A prayer of Moses, the man of God!

¹ Lord,
you have been our eternal accommodation,
from generation to generation.
² Before the mountains were given birth,
before you brought forth the whole earth,
you have been the Everlasting God of worth.
³ You turn people back to dust, henceforth,
Saying , "Mortal man, return back to the earth!"
⁴ A thousand years in your sight,
are like a day, passed by in flight,
or as a watch in the night.
⁵ You carry people to their death and mourning,
like a sleep, forgotten in their forlorning.
They are like the new grass of the dawning dew.
⁶ The morning grass; springs up new.
By evening it's dry and withered through!
⁷ We're consumed, by your angry ruination.
We're terrified, by your indignation.
⁸ You have revelation, of our imperfection.
Your light reveals our sins and transgressions.
⁹ In your wrath, all our days pass away.
We end our days, in groaning dismay.
¹⁰ Our days may come to seventy years,

eighty if our strength endures;
yet the best of them are trouble and sorrow,
for they quickly pass, and we fly on the morrow.
¹¹ How powerful is your anger? If only we knew?
And your wrath,
joined by worship and fear that is due?
¹² Teach us to count our days
and fill our hearts with wisdom, if you may.
¹³ Lord,
how long will it be, before you change your action?
Until you show your servants abundant compassion?
¹⁴ Satisfy us in the morning,
with your unfailing loving ways,
that we may sing for joy, and be glad all of our days.
¹⁵ We've had, many days of affliction,
make us glad, with good years in proportion.
¹⁶ Miracles and wonders are your reputation,
will we see them again in admiration?
Will you show the next generation?
¹⁷ Lord God, show your favour, make us secure.
Work with us, may our work endure.
Create our work and reassure.

Satisfy us in the morning with your unfailing loving ways that we may sing for joy and be glad all of our days

Psalm 91 - Safe and Secure, We Will Endure!

¹ When you live in the shelter, of the Most High.
You rest in the shadow of, El Shaddai.
² I will say of The Lord,
"He is my refuge and my fortress!
He is my God of faithfulness."
³ From the fowler's snare, you will be saved.
He'll rescue you, from the deadly plague.
⁴ His feathers are your protection,
hide under his wings, to avoid detection.
His faithfulness will be your defensive deflection.
⁵ You will not fear the terror of night,
by day no fear of the arrow in flight.
⁶ No fear for disease, that comes under the moon,
nor the plague, that destroys at noon.
⁷ With many thousands dying and disaster all around,
nothing will harm you, as you remain safe and sound.
⁸ As the wicked face punishment and damnation,
you will look on, in observation!
⁹ Because The Lord, is your place to hide,
the Most High, lives right by your side.
¹⁰ You'll sense no evil detection,
safe from plague infection!
¹¹ For he will give his angels charge over you
and guard you; in everything that you do.
¹² With their hands, they lift you, to the safety zone,
so you don't strike your foot against a stone.
¹³ You will tread on the lion and rattlesnake,
trample and crush, without pain or ache!

¹⁴ Then God says,
"Because you acknowledge, I am, 'I Am',
I'll always protect you, with my rescue plan.
¹⁵ I will always answer, when you call.
I'll be with you, in times of trouble.
I'll deliver and honour you all, without a fall.
I'll bless you, with a long life of gratification,
and show you joy in my salvation!"

Psalm 92 – Time to Raise, A Song of Praise
A Sabbath worship song

¹ It's a good and joyful thing,
to give thanks to The Lord, and sing.
Sing praises to, our Most High King!
² We declare your love, at the morning sunrise,
proclaim your faithfulness, under night time skies.
³ Hear the lute, lyre and instruments with string.
Hear the fervent melody ring!
⁴ I see your works and with joy I sing.
I'm shouting, over-flowing, can't keep it in!
I'm exploding!
⁵ Lord, your great deeds are so effective!
Your thoughts are deep and reflective!
⁶ Senseless people in ignorance, remain.
The fool will fail to grasp, though I explain:
⁷ Though the wicked live in prosperity,
they forget that death is their destiny.

They'll be destroyed for eternity!
⁸ Lord, we forever lift you high.
⁹ Surely your enemies can't deny,
that one day they will die!
The sinners will be scattered; will be shattered!
¹⁰ You gave me strength, in your anointing.
Your oil declared; I am your appointing.
¹¹ My enemies are defeated, before my eyes,
their triumph has been denied!
My ears did hear, their surrender cries!
¹² See, the righteous flourish, like a palm tree is able.
Like a cedar, they're strong, majestic and stable!
¹³ Lord, they are grafted, into your house.
In your courtyard they thrive, without doubt.
¹⁴ In their old age, they will still bear fruit,
staying fresh with goodness from the root!
¹⁵ "The Lord is righteous!" They proclaim.
"He is my Rock, with no blame or shame!"

Psalm 93 - The Majesty of Eternity
A song for the end of the week – by King David.

¹ The Lord reigns!
See him dressed, majestic and pure!
He is clothed in majesty, with strength to reassure!
See, the world is fixed, firm and secure!
² Lord, you've reigned as King, from the beginning.
Eternity is your dwelling, in the everlasting!

³ Hear the cacophony; of the mighty sea.
See the mighty oceans; rise up in their devotion.
Waves shout a mighty roar, to the mighty Lord!
The one that they adore!
⁴ He's mightier than the waves, so thunderous!
He's mightier than the breakers, so glorious!
⁵ Lord, you stand firm, in your royal ways.
Holiness decorates your house, for endless days!

Psalm 94
Vengeance Time, Vengeance is Mine
A mid-week song - by King David.

¹ The Lord is the Avenger, of crime.
God, now let your vengeance shine!
It's punish-evil-time!
² Rise up, O Judge, of the earth!
Give to the proud, what they deserve!
³ Lord, how long will the wicked be triumphant?
How long will they boast and be jubilant?
⁴ They spew forth words of arrogance.
Hear the haters brag in ignorance!
⁵ Lord, they crush your people in distress.
Your inheritance they oppress!
⁶ They slay the widow and alien.
They murder the orphaned children.
⁷ They say, "The Lord does not see;

the God of Jacob, just ignores me!"
⁸ Wise up! You stupid ones that despise,
come to your senses, you fools, get wise!
You're bonkers!
Why do you think God denies their cries?
⁹ Let's make this clear, the inventor of the ear,
certainly does hear!
You will also find, the eye he also designed,
and he certainly isn't blind!
Do you even have a clue? He watches all you do!
Do you know it's true?
¹⁰ Does he who disciplines nations,
not punish and chastise?
Does he who teaches mankind,
lack the knowledge of the wise?
¹¹ The Lord knows all human plans, meanwhile,
he knows their resistance is futile!
¹² O Lord, blessed is the one you discipline,
the one you teach from your ruling.
¹³ You grant them relief from distress,
till a pit is dug, for those in wickedness.
¹⁴ As for his people, The Lord, will never relinquish.
His chosen ones, he'll never forsake or extinguish.
¹⁵ To the righteous, justice will return,
and the upright in heart will discern,
they need to follow or burn!
¹⁶ O Lord, who will protect me from the haters?
Who will defend me from the perpetrators?
¹⁷ If The Lord, had not come to help me out,
I would have been dead, without a doubt!

[18] When I screamed, "Lord, I think I'm dying!"
Your unfailing-loving, was my fortifying!
[19] When my anxious mind, was out of control,
your comfort and cheer, soothed my soul.
[20] It's clear you have nothing to do with corruption,
with evil rulers content on disruption.
[21] Against the righteous, the wicked do unite,
condemning the innocent, to death and plight.
[22] But The Lord, has become my strong fortress,
my God the Rock, where I hide from distress!
[23] For their sins it's payback time!
He destroys them for their crime!
They will face God's annihilation,
as he seals their obliteration!

Psalm 95 - Everyone Sing!

[1] Everyone sing, to The Lord of adoration!
Shout it out, to the Rock of our salvation!
[2] Everyone come, our thanks we raise.
We lift him up, with joy and praise!
[3] For The Lord, is the greatest of all,
over other gods, he stands tall!
[4] The depths of the earth are in his grip,
the high mountain peaks in his ownership.
[5] He's the owner of every ocean.

He designed and set the earth in motion!
⁶ Come and worship, God our Creator,
kneel before the King our Maker!
⁷ He is our God, who does provide.
We are his flock, right by his side.
⁸ Listen as he speaks:
"Don't harden your hearts as you did at Meribah!
As you did in the wilderness, that day at Massah!
⁹ When your ancestors tried me and put me to the test,
they could see how good I was, knew I was the best!
¹⁰ For forty years, I grieved their aggravation!
I was disgusted by that wicked generation!
Their hearts crumbled at temptation.
They ignored the ways of our relation
¹¹ In my anger, I declared and made a stand.
They would never enter the Promised Land!
Don't be like them! I hope you understand?"

Psalm 96
Everyone Surrender, to the King of Splendour!

¹ Sing a new song, to The Lord of worth!
Sing to The Lord, all the earth.
² Sing to The Lord and praise his name.
Every day, his salvation we proclaim!
³ Among the nations, declare his glory!
Tell all the people, his miraculous stories.
⁴ For great is The Lord and most worthy of praise!

Be in fear and awe of him always!
⁵ Our Lord God; created the heavenly skies.
The pretentious, false gods are nothing but lies!
⁶ He's preceded by splendour and majesty.
Strength and beauty are his sanctuary.
⁷ Let everyone surrender to The Lord, in delight.
Give to The Lord, glory and might.
⁸ Give his name glory, honour and exalt!
Bring him an offering, into his courts.
⁹ Come worship The Lord, in his holy splendour.
Everyone wait in wonder; tremble and surrender!
¹⁰ To the nations we explain,
that The Lord, does reign!
The world is set firm and squarely,
he'll judge everyone fairly.
¹¹ Let the heavens, be glad and the earth rejoice.
Let the oceans and its dwellers, roar as one voice!
¹² Let the fields and all within, shout in exultation.
Let the trees of the forest,
sing with joyful exclamation!
¹³ Let all creation; praise The Lord, in excess!
He judges the world in righteousness,
and the peoples in his faithfulness.

Let everyone surrender to the Lord, in delight

Give to the Lord glory and might

Psalm 97 - The Lord Reigns Over All
A psalm of David.

¹ The Lord reigns, let the earth delight;
let the distant shores rejoice and ignite!
² His dark, mysterious clouds do surround.
On righteousness and justice, his throne is found!
³ A blazing fire, is his scout,
consumes his enemies all about!
⁴ The world lights up, with his lightning strike.
The earth sees and trembles, in his sight.
⁵ Before The Lord, mountains melt,
like wax in the heat;
when The Lord, of all the earth draws near to meet.

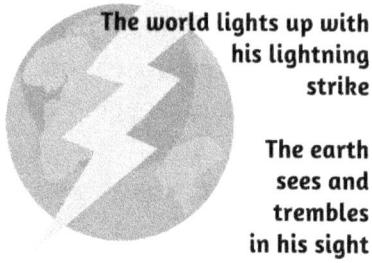

The world lights up with his lightning strike

The earth sees and trembles in his sight

⁶ His righteousness is heaven's proclamation.
People everywhere, see his glorification!
⁷ Let all who worship images; be put to shame.
You false gods and idol worshippers,
fall before his name.
⁸ Zion hears and rejoices!
The villages of Judah have gladness in their voices,
Lord, because of your judgment, choices!
⁹ Over all the earth, you're The Lord Most High.

Far above all false gods, we exalt and magnify!
¹⁰ If you love The Lord, then hate wickedness!
For he, guards his children of faithfulness.
¹¹ On the righteous, he shines his light,
and joy, on those whose heart is upright!
¹² Rejoice in The Lord,
you who are righteous without blame.
Give thanks and praise his holy name!

Psalm 98 – Sing-Along to a New Song
A poetic Psalm of David

¹ Sing to The Lord, a song that's new,
for he has done marvelous things for you!
His right hand and his holy limb (arm),
have worked salvation for him.
² The Lord has made known, his salvation,
and shown his righteousness to the nations.
³ He never forgets his loving faithfulness to Israel,
the salvation of God; seen on a planetary scale!
⁴ Shout for joy to The Lord, all the earth always!
Explode with jubilant songs of praise!
⁵ With the harp, our praises, we are bringing,
with the harp and the joyful sound of singing.
⁶ Let the shofar and trumpet sound!
Echo the triumph of The Lord and King, all around!
⁷ Let the ocean waves; shout with praise!
Let everyone, God's anthem raise!

Singing: "Glory to the King!
Our praises we do sing!"
⁸ Hear the rivers clap in celebration.
The mountains sing a standing ovation
Hear their joyful acclamation!
⁹ When our God of Justice comes,
the world will declare.
He is the world's upright Judge,
treats every person fair!

Psalm 99 - God of Holiness

¹ The Lord reigns!
In fear the nations tremble and shake.
He's enthroned above the cherubim,
let the whole earth quake!
² The Lord in Zion is great!
Over all the nations, we do elevate!
³ Let them, praise your great name.
Awesome and holy, they do proclaim.
⁴ Our Mighty King, love his justice thrall.
He established fairness for all.
He is just and right in Israel.
⁵ Exalt The Lord our God, worship him alone.
He is great and holy, so bow before his throne!
⁶ Moses, Aaron and other priests did proclaim.
Samuel, was among those who called his name.

The Lord heard their cry, and he did reply.
⁷ He spoke to them from the pillar of cloud;
they kept his statutes and decrees he avowed.
⁸ The Lord God of forgiveness,
answered when they pray;
yet he punished them, when they went astray.
⁹ At his holy mountain,
worship The Lord, in exaltation!
Holy is our Lord God, worthy of adoration!

Psalm 100 - Praise The Lord!

A Psalm for thanksgiving

¹ Shout for joy to Yahweh!
People all over the world, don't delay!
² With gladness, worship Yahweh.
Come before him with joyful songs today!
³ Yahweh is God, do you realise?
We're his, because he made us; so open your eyes!
We are his people, his pleasure prize!
⁴ Enter his gates with thanksgiving,
into his courts, with praise and singing.
Give thanks and bless his name,
with the songs that you are bringing!
⁵ For Yahweh is good,
his love endures forever and tomorrow.
His faithfulness endures,
through all generations to follow!

Psalm 101 – Blameless Existence

A poetic Psalm of David

1 I will sing of your love and just ways.
To you, LORD, I will sing praise.
2 I will be careful to lead a blameless existence.
With a blameless heart,
I run the affairs of my residence.
Don't be distanced; when will I see your appearance?
3 My eyes will reject; anything wicked and untrue.
I'll hate and have no part, in what faithless people do!
4 A perverse heart; from me will depart.
I'll rebuke all that's nefarious,
and shun all the iniquitous!
5 The secret, slanderer of my friends,
will be eliminated!
The proud and arrogant; shall not be tolerated!
6 My closest friends,
will be those who are faithful and pure.
The one whose walk is blameless,
will minister and reassure.
7 No deceivers will live in my residence.
No flattering liar; will stand in my presence.
8 All the wicked of the land, I will silence, at sunrise.
From God's city, I eliminate the wicked and despised!

Psalm 102 – Sorrow to Joy

A lament before The Lord – For who are weak, afflicted, overwhelmed and discouraged, open your heart.

¹ Lord, can you hear my prayer? Please reply!
Listen, don't block up my cry!
² Don't hide your face from me, when I'm in trouble.
Listen when I call! Answer at the double!
³ For my days are like smoke, gone in a flash;
my bones burn, like glowing ash.
⁴ My heart is like a withered plant, in the heat.
I am so ill, that I forget to even eat.
⁵ Hear my distressing, loud groans!
I'm nothing left, but flesh and bones!
⁶ I'm like a desert vulture,
like an owl amongst a ruined culture.
⁷ I have no friends, I lie wide awake,
a lone bird on a roof, is this my fate?
⁸ All day long my enemies mock me, taunt and worse;
the wicked haters use my name as a curse!
⁹ I eat my ash of mourning.
I drink my tears of scorning!
¹⁰ Your fury and anger, I do reap.
You grab me and throw me, on the heap!
¹¹ My days are dying, like the evening sun.
Like a withering plant, I am useless scum!
¹² But you, LORD, sit enthroned forever more;
through all generations, your renown endures!
¹³ Show compassion on Zion, it's time to arise.

Show favour, it's time to end their demise!
14 Your servants mourn for Zion's stones.
Her dust moves them, to pitiful groans.
15 The name of The Lord;
will be feared by the nations.
The world's kings, will revere your glorification!
16 The Lord, will appear in glory,
rebuilding all Zion's territory, all hunky-dory!
17 He responds to the destitute cries.
He answers prayer and doesn't despise.
18 Write all this down, for future generations.
The Lord, will be praised, through procreation!
19 The Lord, looked down, from his high abode,
from heaven he did behold, the whole world globe.
20 He heard the prisoners' groans,
as they longed to be free.
He released the death row inmates, from captivity.
21-22 In Jerusalem, people declare God's name.
When the kingdom people gather,
they will praise, The Lord again!
23 He took my strength away, leaving me in sorrow.
He cut short my days, took away, my tomorrow.
24 I cry out,
"I don't want to die, spare me my expiration!
Your years stretch, throughout all generations!
25 In the beginning you laid the earth's foundation,
the heavens are also, the work of your creation.
26 They will perish, but still you remain.
Like clothing they wear out and are changed.
Thrown out and not retained!

²⁷ Yet you remain; the same.
Your years continue and never drain!
²⁸ Our descendants will live with you and continue;
their children will be established before you.

Psalm 103
The Father's Heart, Will Not Depart
A Psalm of David

¹ With my whole being, I praise his holy name.
Praise The Lord, my soul does exclaim!
² Praise The Lord, for my soul's celebration!
I remember your miraculous deeds and reputation!
³ You forgive all my sin, O so much;
cure diseases with your healing touch.
⁴ My life, you did save, from the grave.
Your love crown is your fashion,
you wear it with compassion.
⁵ You grant my desire of goodness, to satisfy.
You give me youthful vigour, like the eagle in the sky!
⁶ The Lord, brings his righteousness
and justice, for all of the oppressed.
⁷ Moses, knew God's way.
The Israelites; saw his deeds display.
⁸ The Lord, is compassionate and gracious,
slow to anger and rich in love for us.
⁹ He won't always make accusations.
He'll never stay angry for infination.

¹⁰ Our sins deserve punishment, more than he gives.
His treatment doesn't match our iniquities.
¹¹ For as high as the heavens are above the ground,
so great is his love for those who fear and bow down!
¹² As far as the east is from the west,
he deletes how we transgress.
¹³ As a father has compassion for his kin,
so The Lord, has kindness on those who fear him.
¹⁴ For he knows how we are designed,
from dirt, he remembers, in his mind.
¹⁵ As for man, his days are few,
like creation's beauty, just passing through!
¹⁶ We're not here long and then we're gone,
no memories left, to dwell upon,
but from everlasting to everlasting.
¹⁷ The Lord's love surrounds those fearing him,
His righteousness is with their children's kin.
¹⁸ You are dependable, to all who keep your way,
they remember your instructions to obey.
¹⁹ The Lord in heaven, has established his throne.
His kingdom rules all known, in every zone.
²⁰ Praise The Lord, you angels, you do as he does say.
You powerful ones, hear his word; then you obey.
²¹ Praise The Lord, you angelic squad,
servants who do the will of God.
²² Praise The Lord, for all he does,
throughout his domain.
Praise The Lord, O my soul,
praise him again and again!

Psalm 104
The Maker Cares, The Maker Shares

¹ My soul will praise The Lord and King!
My Lord God, your greatness is astonishing!
Your clothes of splendour and majesty,
are overwhelming!
² The Lord; wears a garment of light.
He stretches out the curtain of heavenly delight.
³ In the heavenly waters loom,
the beams of the upper room.
From clouds, his chariot is made.
On the wings of the wind he is conveyed.
⁴ The winds, he makes his message supplier.
His servants are the flames of fire.
⁵ He set the earth on its foundation,
firm for future generations.
⁶ All over the earth, the water surged,
oceans covered mountains, submerged.
⁷ At the boom of your voice, the water obeyed,
the thunderous sound, drove the water away.
⁸ The mountains went high and the valleys low,
to the place, you told them to go.
⁹ You set a boundary, where the waters remain,
they never will cover, the earth again.
¹⁰ In the valleys he made, the rivers parade,
whilst the mountain springs, did cascade.
¹¹ Both man and beast, have water refreshing,
a thirst quenching drink, for everything living.
¹² Beside still waters, are the nesting birds;

from the branches above, their songs are heard.
¹³ He waters the mountains from his upper room.
The earth abounds with fruit to consume.
¹⁴ He makes grass grow for the cattle to chew,
and plants for people to cultivate too.
Food from the earth, brings more value.
¹⁵ You gladden hearts, with delicious wine.
The oil you give, make their faces shine.
The sustaining bread, makes man's heart fine.
¹⁶ The trees of The Lord; have much water granted.
Lebanon Cedars, stand tall where he planted.
¹⁷ There the birds make their nests;
in the juniper, the stork finds its rest.
¹⁸ Wild goats reside, on the mountain high.
The rocky crag is where the badgers do lie.
¹⁹ Even the moon has a reason,
as it marks the seasons.
The setting sun marks the day's completion.
²⁰ You turn off the light and it becomes night.
Then the forest beasts prowl, with delight.
²¹ Lions chase their prey, with a roaring sound.
Their food from God, it does abound.
²² Come sunrise, they hide away,
back to their dens, to lie down all day.
²³ Then man goes to work all day,
happy in his achieving.
He works and toils until evening.
²⁴ O Lord, you made so much, so beautiful,
in wisdom, you made them all.
So many creatures, the earth is full!

Then there's the sea, capacious and spacious.
²⁵ The sea life within is countless,
creatures large and small are boundless.
²⁶ There they go; ships to and fro,
see the gigantic whales, deep below

You made them, for a spectacular show.
²⁷ All creatures look to you for good reason,
you give them food, in due season.
²⁸ You give it to them, and they gather the prize,
as each is satisfied, with abundant supplies!
²⁹ When you hide your face,
they are troubled with dismay,
then when you take their breath away,
they return to dust, after their dying day.
³⁰ They are created, when your Spirit comes around,
and renew the face of the ground.
³¹ May the magnificent glory of The Lord,
endure forever!
From all his creation, may he have joy and pleasure!
³² He can look on the earth and it trembles in disrupt,
as he touches the mountains, an explosion erupts!
³³ I will sing to The Lord, as long as I survive.

I will praise my God while I am alive!
34 May he enjoy my sweet meditation!
I rejoice in The Lord of Creation!
35 May the sinners vanish from the earth,
as you end their days!
O my soul; bless The Lord, our hallelujahs raise!
The Lord God be praised!

Psalm 105 - God's Beautiful Nation

1 In the name of The Lord,
give praise and proclamation!
Make known, all his works, among the nations!
2 Sing to him, sing him songs of praise.
Tell everyone, of his marvellous ways!
3 Fill his holy name with glorification!
Fill the hearts of the God seekers,
with joyful celebration!
4 Remember The Lord's strength, you must chase!
Remember always, to seek his face.
5 Remember the wonders, he has achieved.
Remember the miracles, and judgements he decreed!
6 You, his servants, are Abraham's off-spring,
his chosen ones, that's Jacob's kin.
7 He is The Lord, our God, Yahweh!
His judgements are in the earth, on display!
8 He always remembers, his promise declarations;

the agreement he made, for a thousand generations.
⁹ With Abraham, he made a covenant.
With Isaac, swore an oath, in subsequent.
¹⁰ To Jacob, as a decree, he confirmed,
with Israel, an endless covenant affirmed!
¹¹ He said,
"The land of Canaan, I give as your possession.
It is your inheritance portion."
¹² They were given that promise,
when their numbers were low,
strangers to the land, with no place to go.
¹³ From nation to nation, they did stray,
from kingdom to kingdom, finding the way.
¹⁴ He sheltered them from oppression,
for their sake, punished all kings aggression!
¹⁵ He said, "Don't touch my anointed ones;
no harm to my prophets, shall be done!"
¹⁶ He called down famine on the land,
no food supplies to meet demand.
¹⁷ But God sent a man; to Egypt he gave,
Joseph, who was sold a slave!
¹⁸ His feet bruised with shackles and chain.
His soul held by iron pain.
¹⁹ Until his visionary dream came true,
as he did what God told him to do.
²⁰ The king; issued a decree and set Joseph free.
²¹ He declared him, master of his home,
in charge of everything he owned.
²² In charge of giving princes their instruction.

To the king's advisors, he taught wisdom.
²³ Then Jacob came to Egypt, with his family clan,
he lived there as a foreigner, in the land of Ham.
²⁴ The Lord made his people's blessings grow,
their strength increased, to out-number their foes.
²⁵ The Egyptians; turned to hate God's chosen tribes.
His servants faced treacherous conspiracy vibes!
²⁶ His servant Moses, he did send,
and Aaron chosen to depend.
²⁷ God's signs and wonders, they demonstrated,
the Egyptian lands were devastated!
²⁸ At God's direction, at his command,
a plague of darkness covered the land.
²⁹ Their rivers turned to blood, to testify;
causing all their fish to die.
³⁰ Then they suffered a frog invasion,
even the kings bedroom saw infestation!
³¹ God spoke, then, appeared swarms of flies,
and all types of insects plagued the countryside.
³² He bombarded the land with hail for rain.
He sent lightning strikes, fire and flame!
³³ Their vines and trees were all devastated,
throughout the land, trees obliterated.
³⁴ He spoke again and the locust came,
too many to count, it was insane!
³⁵ They ate up all the vegetation
and devoured the fruit of the nation.
³⁶ Then, in every family, the first child died,
snuffed out the days, from their lives!
³⁷ With silver and gold, Israel was let go,

not one person was too slow!
38 Egypt was glad, when they departed,
the dread of Israel, left them broken-hearted!
39 By day, a covering cloud saw them right,
at night, he gave fire, a source of light.
40 When they asked, he gave quail to satisfy.
He fed them well, as bread fell, from the sky.
41 He smashed the rock and water gushed out,
it flowed like a river in the desert drought!
42 He remembered his holy promise, he had made,
to his servant Abraham, assurance gave.
43 God's chosen ones came forth, singing with glee,
with shouts of joy, they were all set free!
44 He blessed them, with the Canaan nations,
they reaped the harvest of the former population.
45 He did it all, so they keep the rules and the laws.
Hallelujah! Praise The Lord!

Psalm 106 - God of Goodness

1 Hallelujah! Praise The Lord!
Thank you God for your goodness!
There really is no end, to his loving kindness.
2 Look at The Lord's mighty operations,
who can make a justified proclamation?
Who amongst us brings satisfaction,
in their praise declaration?
3 Blessed are those, who keep justice in their sight,

for they hold on tight, to all that is right.
⁴ Remember me Lord,
when you show goodness to your nation.
When you come to visit them,
grant me your salvation!
⁵ That I might share the wealth of your chosen nation,
to experience your joy and jubilation,
and receive your inheritance,
in giving praise and acclamation!
⁶ Our fathers sinned and we now do the same,
we all do wrong and act for wicked gain!
⁷ When our fathers fled Egypt,
your miracles escaped their minds,
they forgot your mercies, so kind.
By the Red Sea, they rebelled and maligned!
God's goodness was declined!
⁸ Yet still he saved them, for the sake of his name.
His mighty power declares his fame.
⁹ He rebuked the Red Sea and it obeyed.
His people crossed on a dry highway!
¹⁰ He saved them from the hand of their foe.
Redeemed from the enemy, he let them go!
¹¹ Their enemy was terrified,
engulfed in water and died,
not a single soul survived!
¹² They saw and believed your every word, so amazed,
then they all burst into songs of praise!
¹³ But they soon forgot all his great deeds,
they did not wait for his plan to proceed.
¹⁴ In the desert they expressed,

their craving and distress.
In the wilderness, they put God to the test.
15 So he gave them as they asked
and answered their pleas.
Then their numbers did decrease,
as he sent a killing disease.
16 They envied Moses, in the camp,
Aaron also, with the High Priest rank.
17 The earth opened up and swallowed Dathan,
it closed over the company of Abiram.
18 Among their followers, fire did blaze,
the flames consumed the wicked, without delay!
19 At Sinai, they made a golden calf,
they worshipped the idol, once it was cast.
20 They exchanged their God, so glorious,
for a grass eating bull, so contrarious!
21 They forgot, they were freed from Egyptian labour,
emancipated by God their Saviour!
22 In the land of Ham, miracles and wonders.
At the Red Sea, saw the enemy go under!
23 God said, their fate was his destruction.
Then Moses, the chosen one, made intercession.
He stopped God's annihilation!
24 Still, they thought God's promises were lies,
the land of Canaan, they despised!
25 They grumbled in their ungratefulness,
closed their hearts to God, in unfaithfulness!
26 With uplifted hands, he swore his reply.
He would cause them all, in the desert to die!
27 He exiles their children, among the nations,

scattered throughout, earth's population.
²⁸ They joined themselves, to the Lord of Horus.
They ate sacrifices to the god of the lifeless!
²⁹ They provoked The Lord's anger,
with their wicked ways,
then he punished them, with a plague!
³⁰ Phineas, the priest, intervened
and judgement was made.
He executed the guilty and the plague, was stayed.
³¹ Because of his righteous endeavour,
Phineas will be remembered forever.
³² They also angered The Lord,
at a stream called 'Strife'.
This resulted in trouble for Moses life!
³³ Against the Spirit of God, they rebelled.
Moses became so furious, he yelled!
He yelled in bitterness, they gave him such stress.
³⁴ They failed to carry out the enemy destruction,
as God, had given them instruction.
³⁵ Instead they fraternised, with the enemy nations.
They copied their dark customs, in collaboration.
³⁶ They worshipped their idols, without a care,
in doing so, they became ensnared!
³⁷ Their small children paid the ultimate price,
as to demon gods, they were sacrificed.
³⁸ They took their off-spring
and made them a blood offering!
To the idols of Canaan, they were sacrificing.
Their bloody land, was desecrating!
³⁹ By their own works, they were defiled,

as prostitutes to idols, they were in denial!
⁴⁰ So The Lord, was furious,
with his peoples' insurrection.
He turned away in disgust, as they faced his rejection!
⁴¹ He gave them into the hands of the heathen nations.
Their foes ruled them, without hesitation.
⁴² Their enemies treated them to oppression;
with tyrannical power and subjection.
⁴³ Many times, God delivered them,
with his salvation.
Yet still they continued, in rebellious determination!
Their destruction was their sin and depravation.
⁴⁴ Yet he took note of their distress,
when he heard them cry and confess.
⁴⁵ For their sake,
he remembered his covenant agreement.
Then out of his great love
he relented, his grievance and treatment.
⁴⁶ Then Israel's captors; began a new mercy chapter,
instead of oppression; showed them compassion.
⁴⁷ Save us, Lord our God, gather us from the nations,
that we may give you gratification.
We will praise your holy name in glorification!
⁴⁸ We will praise The Lord, God of Israel,
again and again!
Let all the people say, "Praise The Lord, amen!"

Collection Five
Psalms of Praise and Word.

Psalm 107
The Endless, Relentless, Love of God!

[1] Give thanks to The Lord!
His goodness, you can depend!
His love will never, ever end!
[2] Let the redeemed of The Lord,
tell their story of liberation,
those he saved from the hand of deprivation.
[3] From dark, powerful lands, he brought them forth,
from the east to the west, to the south to the north!
[4] Some wandered on the desert,
without clear destination.
They found no way to a city for habitation.
[5] They fainted from starvation and being parched dry,
their lives were slipping by,
they thought that they would die.
[6] Then they cried out to The Lord,
in their troubled mess;
and he delivered them from distress!
[7] He led them on a straight path, from the desert zone.
He led them to a city,
where they could make their home.
[8] For The Lord's unfailing love,
let them give thanks and praise.

For mankind, he does miracles that amaze.
⁹ To the longing soul, he brings happiness.
The hungry soul, he fills with goodness!
¹⁰ Some sat in darkness, total darkness restriction,
prisoners, bound in chains of affliction.
¹¹ Against God's instruction, they rebelled and denied,
rejected the plans of God Most High!
¹² So he subjected them to bitter, hard labour.
When they stumbled, none offered helpful favour.
¹³ Then they cried out to The Lord,
in their troubled mess;
 and he saved them from their painful distress!
¹⁴ He brought them out of darkness,
the total darkness restriction.
He broke their bondage chains of affliction.
¹⁵ For The Lord's unfailing love,
let them give thanks and praise.
For mankind, he does miracles that amaze!
¹⁶ He smashes bronze gates, for a prison break;
shatters iron bars for all their sakes!
¹⁷ Some became fools, through rebellious ways;
they suffered affliction, due to iniquitous days.
¹⁸ The sight of food, they did hate,
as they drew near to death's gate.
¹⁹ Then they cried out to The Lord,
in their troubled mess;
 and he saved them from their sorrowful distress!
²⁰ When he spoke his word,
 they were healed and saved.

He rescued them all, from the grave!
[21] For The Lord's unfailing love,
let them give thanks and praise.
For mankind, he does miracles that amaze!
[22] Let them, make sacrifices of thanksgiving.
Let them shout of his deeds, with joyful singing!
[23] Some travelled the seas with a trading notion,
faraway merchants on the mighty ocean.
[24] They saw God's power, in the waters deep,
on the high seas, experienced magnificent deeds.
[25] God stirred up a hurricane, when he spoke,
mighty waves, guaranteed to soak; really no joke!
[26] Sea swelling, ships tossing, to sky rising,
then dropping, to the depths plummeting!
Sailors struggle to keep their stomach in.
They struggle to keep fear at bay,
as peril melts their courage away!
[27] Like drunkards, they were reeling and staggered,
at their wits end and feeling haggard.
[28] Then they cried out to The Lord,
in their troubled mess;
and he delivered them from their distress!
[29] The Lord, responded and the storm was crushed.
The waves calmed to a whisper
and the winds were hushed.
[30] They were glad, with the storm's defeat,
as he guided them to a safe retreat.
[31] For The Lord's unfailing love,
let them give thanks and praise.

For mankind, he does miracles that amaze!
³² Let them exalt him, in the people's congregation.
In the company of the elders,
they praise with adoration!
³³ When he decides, he makes rivers disappear,
flowing springs, turn into a desert sphere.
³⁴ He turns fruitful land into a salty waste;
because of the wicked inhabitants in disgrace.
³⁵ He also turns the desert into watery lakes,
from dry ground, flowing springs he makes.
³⁶ He brings all those facing starvation,
then builds a city for their habitation.
³⁷ They sowed fields and planted vines,
reaped a fruitful harvest after time.
³⁸ He blessed them,
and their numbers greatly increased,
He didn't let their herds decrease.
³⁹ Then their numbers decreased,
and they were made low,
humbled by oppression, tragedy and sorrow.
⁴⁰ He who pours scorn on nobles, powerful and grand;
he causes them to wander in a trackless wasteland.
⁴¹ He lifted the needy out of their infirmity,
he then blessed them with large families!
⁴² The upright see and rejoice,
but all the wicked lose their voice.
Let the one who is wise notice these things.
Let them ponder the deeds of The Lord, all loving!

Psalm 108
A Prayer for God's Help Against Our Adversaries
A poetic psalm of King David

1 O God, my heart is focused and agreeing.
O my soul, I praise God with all my being!
2 Awake, harp and lyre and open your eyes!
I will awaken the dawn sunrise!
After the night; greet daybreak with songs of light!
3 I'll praise you, Lord, among the nations.
I will sing of you among congregations.
4 Your love is enormous, beyond heaven high!
Your incredible faithfulness, reaches the skies!
5 O God, be exalted, throughout the heavens grand.
Let your magnificent glory, shine all over the land!
6 Show that you care; come answer our prayer.
Come with your mighty strength and save.
Deliver those who prayed!
7 God speaks, from his place of holiness,
"I divide the battle spoils, from east to west.
Shechem and Succoth, I will share.
Gilead and Manasseh are mine, I declare!
8 Ephraim is my helmet, producing great fighters.
Judah is my sceptre, yielding kings and law writers.
9 Moab is my washbasin, to be my servant low.
On Edom also, my shoe I throw,
it too will serve me so.
Over Philistia, I shout in victory!"
10 Who will lead me into Petra city?

Who will bring me to Edom proximity?
¹¹ Have we really been rejected?
Will you make our armies affective?
¹² Please help us against the foe.
To trust in man is hollow hope.
¹³ With God, we gain a victory rush.
Our enemies he does trample and crush!

Psalm 109 - God, It's Pay-Back Time!
For public worship -A poetic song by King David

¹ My God, whom I praise; why are you silent always?
² Hear the wicked and deceitful,
they slander and despise. Against me are their cries,
on their tongues of festering lies!
³ The haters attack me without reason.
They surround me with words of poison.
⁴ In return for my friendship,
they accuse me without care.
Yet, I declare; I am a man of prayer!
⁵ For my goodness; they give me wickedness.
For being a good mate; they do nothing but hate.
⁶ Send my enemy some evil, bringing condemnation.
Let them stand near,
with obnoxious lies and accusations!
⁷ When he is judged, let him be found guilty as sin,
may his prayers turn him in!
⁸ Let him have few days to face,

then another shall seize his leadership place!
⁹ Make his children orphans, when you end his life!
A weeping widow, is his mourning wife!
¹⁰ May his children become nomadic tramps!
Vagabonds evicted from their ruined camp!
¹¹ May a creditor seize all he has in favour!
May strangers plunder the fruits of his labour!
¹² May no one extend him kindness of any fashion,
these orphans deserve no one's compassion!
¹³ May he leave no legacy; no posterity!
In the next generation,
may their names face obliteration!
¹⁴ May The Lord remember his father's sins in conceit!
The sins of his mother, God will not delete!
¹⁵ May their sins before The Lord, always remain,
on earth, he will delete their name!
¹⁶ For, he never thought of doing a kind deed.
He hounded to death, the poor,
broken-hearted in need!
¹⁷ Yes, he loves to curse,
may it come back on him and bite!
He didn't want blessings,
they brought him no delight!
¹⁸ Cursing was his garment ornamentation,
it seeped into his body, like water penetration.
It entered his bones, like oil percolation.
²⁰ May his curses be his bondage,
and cause his suffocation.
This will be The Lord's payment remuneration.
²¹ But now, Sovereign Lord,

help me for your name's sake.
Deliver me, out of the goodness of your love so great!
22 For I am poor and in need,
with a wounded heart, I plead.
23 Like an evening shadow, away I fade.
Like a locust, I'm shaken off in a daze.
24 From all the fasting, my knees are weak,
so emaciated, that my bones all creak!
25 My accusers taunt and scorn me in revulsion.
They see me and shake their heads in repulsion!
26 Help me, O my Lord God above!
Save me through your unfailing love.
27 Then everyone will know,
what you have done for me.
Then they will say,
"The power of The Lord gave him victory!"
28 They may curse, yet blessings are your choice.
Please shame those who attack me,
with obscenities in their voice!
As your servant, I always will rejoice!
29 Clothe my demonic accusers,
in disgrace and blame.
May they be wrapped, in a robe of shame!
30 I will lift great praise to The Lord,
with my thankful voice.
In the huge, heaving congregation,
I give him praise and rejoice!
31 For he stands right next to the needy in deprivation.
He saves their lives from those with condemnation!

Psalm 110
My Lord, Messiah and King, My Everything!
A Psalm by King David

[1] The Lord God spoke, to my Lord and Messiah,
"For you to sit right next to me, it is my desire.
Sit there, while I make your enemies
a footstool for your feet."
[2] Then, from Zion,
The Lord with the mighty sceptre did speak,
"Rule in the midst of your enemies shriek!"
[3] On your battle day; your people will be ready to do.
Dressed in magnificent holiness, your youths,
come to you
They spring forth from the morning womb,
like fresh dew!
[4] The Lord won't change his mind,
he swore an oath and says,
"In the order of Melchizedek,
you are a priest always!"
[5] The Lord, who is at your right hand,
on his rage day, will crush kings that are damned!
[6] He will judge the nations with dread;
heaping up the valleys with dead!
Earth's rulers will be crushed and bled!
[7] Yet he will drink from the brook along the way.
He will hold his head high, on that victorious day!

Psalm 111 – Praise and Glorify, Lord Adonai!

¹ Shout your praise, to Lord Adonai!
Hallelujah! Hear my heart cry!
In the upright congregation;
hear heartfelt appreciation!
² The great works of The Lord, are a wondrous sight.
All who seek them, consider them a delight!
³ All that he does is glory and majesty.
His righteousness lasts for eternity.
⁴ His miracles and wonders can't be forgotten.
The Lord is full of grace and compassion.
⁵ Those who fear him, receive his food provision.
He always remembers his covenant decision.
⁶ His people witnessed his powerful deeds operation,
gifting them the lands of the Canaan nation!
⁷ The works of his hands are faithful and just;
all of his rules you can always trust.
⁸ Forever and ever is their steadfastness,
they are built on truth and righteousness.
⁹ He sent redemption, for his people's gain.
His covenant ordained, will always remain.
Holy and awesome is Adonai's name!
¹⁰ The beginning of wisdom; is the fear of Adonai.
All who understand his rules; will comply.
Our praise to him will never die!

Psalm 112
Shout and Celebrate, the Victory of Faith!

¹ Praise The Lord! Let's shout in celebration!
Fear of The Lord;
brings blessings beyond expectation.
His commands bring delightful gratification.
² Their children will be mighty in the nation.
Blessed will be the upright generation.
³ Wealth and riches fill the homes of the wise.
Their integrity and righteousness never dies!
⁴ Even in the darkness, light comes bursting through,
for the righteous are so gracious,
compassionate and true.
⁵ Goodwill comes to those who lend
and generously care,
with justice they conduct their affairs.
⁶ The righteous will never be shaken, never!
Others will remember them forever.
⁷ They will have no dread, fear or anxious worry.
Their hearts are firm in faith, of The Lord's victory!
⁸ Their hearts are secure, no fear does show;
calmly they have triumph on their foes.
⁹ They have freely shared gifts to the poor and needy.
Their righteousness lasts for eternity.
They will be lifted high in honour and dignity.
¹⁰ The wicked will see and be angered severe.
They will gnash their teeth and disappear.
The desire of the wicked will perish from here!

Psalm 113 – Generosity of Lord Adonai

[1] Lord Adonai, we give you praise!
All you servants of The Lord, praise him always.
Keep praising him for all your days!
[2] Praise the name of Adonai, for now and always.
[3] From dawn until dusk,
to praise the name Adonai, is a must!
[4] Over all the nations, exalt The Lord, Adonai.
His glory is greater than the heavenly sky.
[5] No one compares to Lord Adonai.
He is the One enthroned on high!
[6] He stoops to gaze on the earth and sky.
[7] He rescues the poor from the dust bowl.
He lifts the needy from the ash and dung hole!
[8] He gives them a princes' identification.
He sits them with the princes of his nation.
[9] He gives the barren woman a home to occupy.
He gives her children to pacify.
Praise The Lord Adonai!

Psalm 114 – Passover Song

[1] Way back in the past, Israel left Egypt, free at last!
[2] Judah became God's sanctuary,
free from oppression,
whilst Israel became his possession.
[3] The Red Sea looked and away it flew!

Then later, the Jordan River did too.
They moved aside and the people passed through.
⁴ Fear shook the mountain land,
like leaping goats and lambs.
⁵ Why did you, sea; decide to divide?
Why, Jordan, open up inside?
⁶ What frightened the mountains and land?
What caused them to leap, like goats and lambs?
⁷ The earth trembles, in The Lord's wake.
In the presence of Jacob's God,
it trembles and shakes!
⁸ From the rock into streams,
come gushing and roaring.
He changed rock into springs with water pouring!

Psalm 115 - The One Only True God

¹ Not to us, Lord, not to us at all!
To your name, be the glory call!
Because you are Love, so faithful!
² Why do the nations say,
"Where is their God anyway?"
³ Yet we know our God is in heaven, higher.
He does whatever he desires.
⁴ The doubters' idols are work and wealth
and all things made by themselves.
⁵ The idols have mouths, yet voices they cannot find.

They have two eyes, yet still they're blind!
⁶ They have ears, but no hearing.
They have noses, yet smell nothing!
⁷ They have hands, but no feeling sensation.
They have feet, but no ambulation!
Their throats have sound elimination!
⁸ The idols are all dead, just like their makers.
The makers are misled, like all who trust the fakers!
⁹ O Israel,
trust the One True Lord, you are his affection.
He helps you with his shield of protection!
¹⁰ Aaron's priesthood, trust the One True Lord,
you are his affection.
He helps you with his shield of protection!
¹¹ All who fear him, trust the One True Lord,
you are his affection.
He helps you with his shield of protection!
¹² The Lord remembers our every need;
he will bless us indeed!
He blesses Israel, with all things good.
He blesses Aaron's priesthood!
¹³ Those who fear The Lord, he will bless them all.
He treats them all the same, the great and the small.
¹⁴ May The Lord, give you more and more increase,
both you and your children,
will have his blessing piece.
¹⁵ May you be blessed, by The Lord our Maker.
You are blessed by heaven and earth's Creator!
¹⁶ The highest heavens are God's holy place,

but the earth, he has given to the human race.
¹⁷ The dead in the grave; can't give The Lord praise.
The silent deceased; can't let their praise release!
¹⁸ But we praise The Lord, in exaltation!
Both now and for perpetuation!
Lord, accept our praise and celebration!

Psalm 116 - I Am Saved, From the Grave!

¹ I love The Lord Adonai, for he heard my voice!
He heard my cry, when I made my mercy choice.
² Because he listened to my cry;
I will call on him, as long as I'm alive.
³ Death once had its grip on me.
The terror of the grave cost my sanity.
I was overcome by torment and worry.
⁴ Then I called on the name of Adonai,
"Lord, save me! Don't let me die!"
⁵ The Lord, is gracious and upright.
Our God is full of merciful delight.
⁶ The Lord protects the unaware.
When I was low, he saved me and cared!
⁷ O my soul; return to your rest.
The Lord, has been good and done his best.
⁸ O Lord, from death you saved my life,
from tears, you dried my eyes,
kept my feet from a stumbling surprise!
⁹ Before The Lord, I now strive, in his giving.

I can walk in the land of the living.
¹⁰ I trusted God, when I said and persisted,
"Lord, I am so afflicted!"
¹¹ I said, when I was weak,
"Everyone is a lying cheat!"
¹² O Lord, what can I give back to you,
for all my blessings, that you do?
¹³ I will lift up his cup of salvation.
I'll praise his name for my liberation!
¹⁴ I will fulfill to The Lord, my promises;
in the presence of his witnesses.
¹⁵ When a servant of The Lord, dies and departs;
God is saddened, as it touches his heart.
¹⁶ Lord, I truly am your servant to retain.
My mother served you, as do I, I serve your name.
You freed me from my bondage chains!
¹⁷ I sacrifice to you, an offering, for my thankful gain.
O Lord, I call upon your name!
¹⁸ I will fulfill to The Lord, my promises;
in the presence of his witnesses,
despite all of my difficulties.
¹⁹ I will worship you in your courts space,
in Jerusalem, in your temple place!
O Lord, it is you that I praise!

Psalm 117
The Lord be Praised, for Endless Days!
A Psalm of praise

¹ Praise The Lord, all you nations!
Everyone praise him, in exaltation!
² His mercy and love to us is great.
The Lord has never ending faith!
So praise The Lord and celebrate.
The Lord be Praised; for Endless Days!

Psalm 118 – Thanks for Glory, Thanks for Victory!
A Psalm of praise

¹ Give thanks to The Lord, he is good and sure!
His love will for ever endure!
² Let all of Israel say,
"His love will never fade away!"
³ Let Aaron's priesthood sing,
"His love is everlasting!"
⁴ Hear those who fear The Lord and do depend,
"His love will never end!"
⁵ I cried to The Lord, when hard pressed,
I cried in my distress.
He brought me to a special place,
with freedom and so much space.
⁶ The Lord is with me; I shall not fear.

No one can hurt me, when The Lord is near.
7 The Lord, helps me, in his delivery,
upon my enemy, I look down, in victory!
8 O Lord, your protection is better for certain,
it's better than a human person!
9 O Lord, it's better to seek your protection;
than that of a royal princely connection!
10 I was once surrounded by all the nations,
in the name of The Lord, I beat them to capitulation!
11 They surrounded me on every side,
in the name of The Lord, I cut them down to size!
12 Like angry bees, around me they swarmed,
yet, were consumed as quickly as burning thorns!
13 I was pushed back and about to fall,
then The Lord, gave me victory, over them all!
14 The Lord defends me from condemnation.
He is my strength and my salvation!
15 We now hear the victory shout,
as songs of joy do ring out.
Every righteous heart and in their homes, they sing.
The Lord's right hand; has done mighty things!
16 The Lord's right hand is lifted highly!
"The Lord's right hand has done things mighty!"
17 I will not die, but live and overcome.
I will proclaim what The Lord has done!
18 The Lord has punished me severely;
but he will never kill me.
19 Swing wide the righteous gates!
I will enter with thanks, for The Lord is great!
20 For this is The Lord's gate;

where the righteous enter and celebrate!
²¹ I thank you, for answered prayer communication.
You are my delivering salvation!
²² The builder's rejected stone,
has become the cornerstone.
²³ The Lord has made this be; it is marvellous to see!
²⁴ This is the day that The Lord created,
let us rejoice and celebrate it!
²⁵ Lord, save us and set us free!
Lord, grant us success and victory!
²⁶ The one who comes,
in the name of The Lord, is blessed!
We bless you from within the temple fortress!
²⁷ For The Lord our God,
has given us his illumination,
with leafy branches, join the festival procession,
to the altar with your sacrificial expression!
²⁸ You are my God, I praise and rejoice
You are my God; I exalt you with my voice!
²⁹ Give thanks to The Lord, he is good and sure!
His love will for ever endure!

This is the day that the Lord created let us rejoice and celebrate it!

Psalm 119 – God's Word Must be Heard!

This Psalm is one of several acrostic poems found in the Bible. Its 176 verses are divided into 22 stanzas, one for each of the 22 characters that make up the Hebrew alphabet, from א Aleph to ת Taw

א Aleph - The Way of Blessings

¹ Blessed are the blameless, with sincerity.
They follow the light of God's Word, with integrity!
² Blessed are those who follow his statutes,
with all their heart, it's him that they pursue!
³ They do no wrong, never go astray.
They always do right and follow his way.
⁴ God gave us rules and he did say,
"I need you to fully obey!"
⁵ Oh, that my ways were steadfast indeed,
that I could obey all of your decrees!
⁶ Then I would have no shame,
for I keep your commands, they will remain.
⁷ With an upright heart I give you praise;
as I learn your righteous ways.
⁸ I will obey your decrees and laws.
Do not forsake me at all!

ב Beth - Joyous Truth

⁹ How can a young person stay pure in what they do?
Only by following God's Word and what is true!
¹⁰ With all my heart, I seek your direction.
Don't let me wander from your instruction!
¹¹ Your Word is in my heart, buried deep within,

so against you, I might not sin.
¹² Praise be; to you, O Lord of Truth!
Teach me the power of your statutes!
¹³ From within my lips, I speak out.
I recount all the laws that come from your mouth.
¹⁴ I rejoice in following your decrees;
as one rejoices in being wealthy.
¹⁵ I give your laws my meditation.
To your ways, I show consideration.
¹⁶ Your decrees bring me such delight.
I will always keep your Word in my sight!

ג Gimel - Life in Abundance

¹⁷ Give this servant life in abundance;
that I may obey your Word and it's guidance.
¹⁸ Open my eyes, that I may observe;
the wonderful things, hidden in your Word.
¹⁹ For a brief time on earth, I will reside.
I need your commands, so please don't hide.
²⁰ I have a constant, burning desire,
for your laws every time I require!
²¹ You rebuke the arrogant, they are cursed,
they ignore your commands, in your word.
²² The mockers scorn, please take it away!
Your statutes, I will always obey!
²³ Rulers may slander me, with words of hate.
Yet, this servant, on your decrees, will meditate!
²⁴ Your statutes are my delight!
They're my counsellors, for an abundant life!

ד Daleth – Revive Me by Your Word!
²⁵ I lay crushed, in the dust, feeling perturbed.
Do as you promised, revive me by your Word!
²⁶ I confessed my life and you answered me.
Please teach me your holy decrees!
²⁷ I need to understand, the way of your commands.
Your deeds and exploitations;
deserve my meditations.
²⁸ Sadly my soul is struggling to survive.
According to your Word, you strengthen and revive.
²⁹ Save me from deceit and everything false.
Graciously keep me true to your laws.
³⁰ The way of faith is my destination.
To your laws, I give my whole concentration!
³¹ Lord, your statutes in me, always remain.
Don't let me be put to shame!
³²I follow the way of your commands.
For you have helped me to understand!

ה He – Give Me An Understanding Heart
³³ Give me revelation about your ways;
that I may follow it always!
³⁴ Give me a heart to understand;
that I may obey your every command!
³⁵ Guide me on the path of your obedience;
there I find a delightful experience!
³⁶ Turn my heart to your Word, let it remain;
and not to rich and wealthy gain!
³⁷ Shield my eyes from deceptions and absurd;
save my life, according to your Word!

³⁸ Keep your promises as they are true.
I'm your servant, in fear, I bow before you!
³⁹ Save me from the dread and disgrace,
for I believe your Word is great!
⁴⁰ My desire is to obey,
the commandments of your way!
Let your Spirit upright; give me a new life!

ו Waw – Trust The Lord, Trust the Word!
⁴¹ Come Lord, your love never fails me.
Your salvation and promises set me free
⁴² Then, I can respond, to the mockers in disgust,
as in your Word, I do trust!
⁴³ Let your words of truth always be in my mouth.
In your law, I have hope and no doubt!
⁴⁴ I will observe your laws every day
and never forget the words you say.
⁴⁵ I will live in freedom perfection,
as I aim to follow in your direction.
⁴⁶ I will speak of your truths to kings that reign
and will not be put to shame!
⁴⁷ My pleasure and delight is in your Word.
I love it, when you speak and I have heard!
⁴⁸ I reach out for more of your Word
and truth revelation.
Upon your instruction, I love more truth meditation!

ז Zayin - My Hope and Comfort

49 Lord, always remember what you promised to do.
Your promises bring hope and my comfort too.
50 My comfort in my suffering is sufficed!
Your promises gave me life.
51 I am mocked by the arrogant unmerciful.
Yet, I never give up on your law.
52 Your ancient laws help me to cope,
they encourage me with comfort and hope!
53 When I see the wicked, breaking your commands,
I fill with anger and need to make a stand!
54 My life is a journey, of words and melody.
I sing joyous songs, about your decrees.
55 Lord, through the night,
your name is on my thoughts.
So I keep and declare your laws!
56 I have practiced and observed,
to obediently follow your Word!

ח Heth - Devotion to Instruction

[57] You are my everything, O lord!
I have promised to obey your laws.
[58] With all my heart, I seek your face.
Remember you promised, to show me grace!
[59] When I know that I have gone astray,
I turn back to your instructions and obey.
[60] I have considered my life direction.
I pledge to follow your instruction.
61 So I hurry, without delay.

Your commands I will obey!
61 When the wicked trap me with temptation,
I remember your law brings liberation!
62 I give you thanks, in the middle of the night,
for all your laws are true and right!
63 I'm a friend to all who serve you,
to all who follow your Word of truth!
64 O Lord,
the earth is filled with your love continuation!
Give me more commandments revelations!

ט Teth – The Greatest Treasure, Gives Me Pleasure
[65] Your promises Lord, you have kept them true.
You've been good to me, in all you do!
[66] Give me your knowledge and wisdom,
for I trust the commands of your Kingdom!
[67] I used to do wrong, before your correction,
now, I see your wisdom direction.
[68] You are so good; you're good and kind.
Show me your commands, transform my mind!
[69] With lies, the arrogant slander me.
Yet, I passionately follow all your decrees!
[70] Their hearts are dull, with no feeling at all,
but I find treasure in your law.
71 It was good for me to face correction,
so I might learn your direction!
72 When you speak your law, it's the greatest treasure.
All the money is the world,
will not give such pleasure!

׳ Yodh – Life-Giving Law

⁷³ You made and formed me with your hands.
Help me to understand,
 to learn more of your commands.
⁷⁴ May those who trust you,
rejoice when they see me like this.
For I have my heart, in your hope and promise.
⁷⁵ O Lord, I know that your laws are up right,
even when you punished me, to set me right!
⁷⁶ Comfort me, with your unfailing love, so good!.
Remember you made me a promise you would.
⁷⁷ Let your compassion save my life!
In your life-giving law, I do delight!
⁷⁸ Let the arrogant know shame and humiliation,
they oppressed me without causation.
On your instruction, I turn to meditation!
⁷⁹ May those who trust you come to me;
as I understand and follow your decrees.
⁸⁰ Help me,
to totally follow your decrees and declarations.
So spare me the shame and humiliation!

כ Kaph – Salvation Conversation

⁸¹ I'm exhausted, waiting for your salvation.
In your Word, I put hopeful expectation!
⁸² As I look for your promise, my eyes fail to see.
I ask, "When will you comfort me?"
⁸³ Like a dried-out wineskin, my soul is squeezed!
I'll always remember your decrees.
⁸⁴ How long must I wait? How much time?

Will you punish my persecutors, for their crime?
⁸⁵ The arrogant men, who disobey your law,
dig their pits, to make me fall!
⁸⁶ Help me! I'm persecuted without cause.
Yet, I still trust in all your laws!
⁸⁷ They've almost succeeded in killing me.
Yet, still I follow your decrees!
⁸⁸ In your unfailing love, revive me in salvation!
That I may obey the rules of your conversation!

ל Lamedh - Faith in God's Word
⁸⁹ O Lord, your Word will never die!
It stands firm in the heavens high!
⁹⁰ Your faithfulness endures for all generations.
You established all of creation,
a miracle of continuation.
⁹¹ To this day, all things endure,
because of your Word.
For you made them for your glory and to serve!
⁹² If your law had not been my source of gain,
I would have perished in my suffering pain.
⁹³ I always remember your instructions,
they provide my life with preservation.
⁹⁴ Lord, I am yours, for your salvation.
Your laws have been my realisation.
⁹⁵ The wicked are lurking for my destruction.
Yet, still I consider your instruction.
⁹⁶ I know perfection, has its limitation.

Yet your perfect Word; exceeds all expectation!

מ Mem - I Love God's Word
97 Your law is a loving treasure chest,
I always think about it and am blessed!
98 Your commands are with me always.
I'm wiser than the foe that prey.
99 I know more than those who teach me,
for I meditate on your decrees.
100 I know more than the elders and understand,
for I obey all of your commands.
101 I have avoided the path of evil temptation.
I have given your Word, obedient observation
102 From your truth, I have no separation,
for you taught me in preparation.
103 Your Word tastes sweet and yummy.
In my mouth it's sweeter than honey!
104 Your truth is the source that makes me wise,
so all the false paths, I do despise!

נ Nun – Shine Your Light of Truth
105 Your Word is a lamp to guide upon my trail,
a light on my path that never fails!
106 I've taken an oath and confirmed it all,
I've said, "I will follow your righteous law!"
107 I have suffered much, will my life preserve?
Lord, give me life, according to your Word!
108 O Lord, receive my thanks and praise.
Then teach me more of your ways.
109 Though I'm ready to face destruction,

I'll keep on following your instruction.
[110] The wicked set a trap of temptation.
Yet, from your truth, I show no deviation!
[111] Your Word is a legacy, it will never depart.
It brings joy, to fill my heart!
[112] My heart will always keep your decrees,
throughout all eternity!

ס Samekh - Safe in God's Word
[113] Your law? I love it and adore.
Yet, double-minded people; I hate and abhor!
[114] You're my refuge and my shield.
In your Word, my hope is revealed!
[115] All you sinful people get away!
You can't stop me following my God's way!
[116] My God! You promised to sustain my life!
Don't let my hopes be dashed and wiped!
[117] Uphold me and I will be saved.
I will always pay attention to your ways.
[118] You reject the fools that ignore your laws,
their deceitful plans are no use at all!
[119] The wicked are trash, without worth,
that is why I love your Word!
[120] My body trembles in fear of you.
I stand in awe of your Word so true!

ע Ayin - I Obey Your Ways
[121] I've done what is just and right.
Don't leave me to the hater's plight!
[122] Promise that you'll break me free.

Don't let the arrogant oppress me!
¹²³ My eyes fail, in anticipation, for your salvation,
for your righteous promise of emancipation!
¹²⁴ Treat me according to your loving way.
Instruct me how to obey.
¹²⁵ As I serve, help me to understand,
that I may know more of your commands!
¹²⁶ O Lord, it's time for you to do more,
for the haters ignore, your law!
¹²⁷ Your commands I love and behold,
more than twenty-four karat gold.
¹²⁸ So I follow all your instructions.
I hate to go in the wrong direction!

פ Pe - Desire to Obey, The Lord's Way
¹²⁹ You have a wonderful way.
With all my heart, I do obey.
¹³⁰ The revealing of your Word brings light.
The ignorant receive wisdom and insight.
¹³¹ I open my mouth with such deep panting.
I desire and need your commanding.
¹³² Show me mercy, turn to me again,
as you do to the lovers of your name.
¹³³ Provide me with your promise filled direction,
save me from sinful dominion.
¹³⁴ Give me redemption, from the hater's oppression,
that I will follow your instruction.
¹³⁵ Shine on me, as I serve
and teach me more of your Word.
¹³⁶ I cry in an uncontrollable way,

when I see your law being disobeyed!

צ Tsadhe - His Word Is Just, In It We Trust
^{137} O Lord, your laws are right and just!
^{138} Your righteous laws, we totally trust!
^{139} I passionately fight, to do what's right,
still the haters ignore your Word in spite!
140 Your promises are certain and assured,
that is why, I love your Word.
141 Though I'm lowly and despised,
your teachings I will not deny!
142 Your righteousness will never end,
your law is true, we can depend.
143 Trouble and distress are now my plight.
Yet your commands, bring me delight.
144 Your instructions are always right and just.
Give me understanding, to live and trust.

ק Qoph – Help!
^{145} Lord, with all my heart I plea,
I will obey your decrees.
^{146} I cry out for me to save,
I will follow your every way.
^{147} Before dawn, I cry for help
and wrap your Word into myself.
^{148} Every night, I lie awake,
on your promises I meditate.
^{149} In your love continuation,
hear my cry of deprivation.
Lord, give my life, your mercy preservation!

¹⁵⁰ Nearby the haters scheme and devise!
They are far from your law they all despise!
¹⁵¹ You are near Lord, your commands are true.
¹⁵² Long ago I learned from your statutes.
Established forever by you!

ר Resh - Give Me Life!
¹⁵³ My suffering, you see and deliver me,
for I remember all your decrees!
¹⁵⁴ Save me with your great redemption.
You promised me your death protection!
¹⁵⁵ The wicked are far from your salvation,
they disobey your laws, without hesitation!
¹⁵⁶ O Lord, your compassion is massive.
According to your laws, my life you give.
¹⁵⁷ Many are the foes that now attack.
Yet from your ways, I will not turn back.
¹⁵⁸ In disgust, I look at those with no faith,
they ignore your Word with such hate!
¹⁵⁹ Lord, through your unchanging love,
save me from destruction,
for I do truly love, all of your instructions.
¹⁶⁰ Your Word is truth on it depend.
Your righteous ways will never end!

ש Sin and Shin - Commitment to God's Word
¹⁶¹ The powerful persecute, without provocation.
At your Word, my heart trembles with vibration!
¹⁶² In your promise I rejoice,
happy with a treasure chest of choice!

163 I hate and despise, and detest all lies,
but I love and obey, all of your ways.
164 Seven times each day, I praise you,
for all your righteous statutes!
165 Great peace, have all, who love your law,
nothing will make them stumble and fall.
166 Lord, I long for your salvation,
your Word is my dedication.
167 I obey your statutes; my love for them is huge!
168 I follow your instructions and commands,
for you see all I do with my hand!

ת Taw - I Cry For Your Help

169 Lord, let my cry for help reach you.
Give me understanding, as you promised to do!
170 Listen to my heartfelt prayer.
You promised to save me and care!
171 Let my lips overflow with praise,
for you teach me all your ways!
172 I sing of your Word in delight,
for all of your commands are right.
173 Be ready to help me with your hand,
for I have chosen your commands.
174 Lord, save me from my plight,
for your law gives me such delight!
175 Let me live and give you praise,
may you sustain me with your ways!
176 Like a lost sheep, I stray the land.
Search for me, for I remember your commands!

Psalm 120 - God Hear My Prayer
A song to ascend

¹I called to The Lord, with a troubled cry.
He did hear and then replied!
²Lord, come to me with your salvation.
Save me from deceit and false accusation!
³What will God do to you liars?
How will he punish the deniers?
⁴He'll pierce you with arrows of condemnation,
and consume you with coals of damnation!
⁵Living with the ones that have damned
and slammed,
is as bad as living in a savage land!
Is this my destination plan?
⁶I've lived with the peace-haters, for far too long.
⁷I speak as a peace-maker; they're for war and wrong!

Psalm 121 - God Our Protector
A song to ascend

¹I look to the mountains and ask,
"Where's my liberation?"
²My help comes from, The Lord of all Creation!
He is my protection!
³He will not let me fall!
He's always awake and hears my call.
Never does he ignore.

⁴ The protector of Israel; never dozes, sleeps or fails.
⁵ God is your guard, with him you're allied.
He will always protect you by his side.
⁶ You'll know no harm in the sunlight,
or face danger under the moon at night.
⁷ The Lord, protects you from all kinds of strife.
He keeps you safe and saves your life.
⁸ The Lord, protects as you come and go,
both now and forever, it is so!

Psalm 122 – Praise for Jerusalem

A song to ascend by King David

¹ I rejoiced when I heard them say,
"Let's go to the house of Yahweh."
² Now here we are on Jerusalem land,
inside your gates, we now stand!
³ O Jerusalem, built as a city of praise.
It's where God meets man, any days.
⁴ Everyone goes there, every tribe.
They worship The Lord, with their praise vibe.
To his commands, they do ascribe!
It's where kings do condemn and condone.
⁵ It's where the house of David, established his throne.
⁶ Pray for the peace of Jerusalem city:
"May those who love you know prosperity!
⁷ O Jerusalem, may there be peace inside your walls,

and safety in your palace halls."
⁸ For all my family that do live there,
I offer my intercession prayer.
"Show them your peace and care!"
⁹ For the sake of your house, our God, dwelling there;
I seek Jerusalem's prosperity and welfare!

Psalm 123 – Mercy Prayer
A song to ascend

¹ God, I look to you in your heavenly home.
I worship you who sits on the throne.
² As a servant looks to a master and does depend.
Like a maid looks to her mistress, she attends.
So our eyes look to you Lord, again and again.
Until your mercy, you do send.
³ Have mercy, O Lord, don't make us exempt,
for we have endured, so much contempt!
⁴ Constant sneering and jeering,
the mocking and scoffing, so loud!
Ridicule from the rich, wealthy, arrogant and proud!

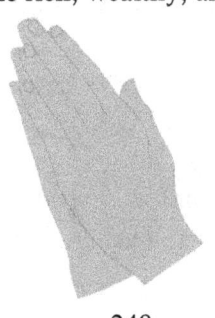

Psalm 124 – Glorious Victorious
A song to ascend by King David

[1] What if God was not on our side?
Then all of Israel replied!
[2] "What if God, had not been there for us?
When our enemies were violent and dangerous!
[3] They would have swallowed us alive.
Their fury against us did arise!
[4] We would have drowned in the flood so huge,
and been swept away in the deluge!
[5] Washed away in the deadly torrent,
in the raging waters so abhorrent!"
[6] Praise God, he never went away,
he kept all our enemies at bay!
[7] From the fowler's snare we escaped like a bird.
The trap was destroyed, we dodged being captured!
[8] From The Lord, comes victory and salvation.
He is our Maker, Lord of all Creation!

Psalm 125 - God's Surrounding Protection
A song to ascend

[1] Those who trust in The Lord,
are like Mount Zion, so sure.
It cannot be shaken but forever endures!
[2] As the mountains surround Jerusalem's walls,
so The Lord,

surrounds his people, now and evermore.
³ Over the land of the righteous,
the ruling wicked shall depart,
for if they don't depart;
the righteous might turn to the evil arts.
⁴ Lord, do right, to those who are upright,
to those who obey your way, with delight!
⁵ But those who turn to wicked avail,
The Lord will abandon them and prevail!
Peace be on Israel!

Psalm 126 - Restored
A song to ascend

¹ The fortunes of Zion were restored,
by our Mighty Redeeming Lord.
Like we were in a dream, or so it seemed!
² We had a kind of laughing, smiling, gladness phase.
Then we shouted joyous songs of praise.
Then, word spread on the nation's grapevine,
"For them, The Lord, did mighty fine!"
³ The things The Lord, did for them was great!
Overflowing with joy, they did celebrate!
⁴ Lord, make us prosper again,
as you fill dry river beds with rain!
⁵ Those who weep, as they sow their seed,
they reap their harvest, with joyful glee.
⁶ They're weeping as they go;

carrying seed that they will sow.
Then they return feeling blessed.
Sing joyful songs for an abundant harvest!

Psalm 127 - His Delightful Gifts
A song to ascend by Solomon

[1] Unless The Lord, builds the house,
the builders labour in vain.
Unless he watches over the city,
for the watchmen it is the same!
[2] It really is crazy to work this way,
from sunrise till the end of day!
They toil in fear, of not enough food to eat.
Yet, God provides for the trustworthy,
when they sleep!
[3] Children are a gift from The Lord;
they are a generous reward.
[4] The number of children, born to a young man,
are like the number of arrows, in a soldier's hand.
[5] Blessed is the man whose quiver is full!
With a house full of children, he will never fall.
He will beat his opponent,
in the judgement court hall!

Psalm 128 - The Reward of The Lord
A song to ascend

¹ Blessed are they, who obey The Lord;
who live in obedience to his Word!
² Your hard work will provide your reward.
Prosperous blessings are your accord.
³ Inside your home, your wife will provide.
Your joyful children gather at your table side.
⁴ Yes, the man who fears The Lord,
will be blessed with this reward!
⁵ May The Lord, bless you from Zion;
may you see the prosperity of Jerusalem,
for all your life to come.
⁶ May you live to see your grandchildren.
May your rewards never cease!
Let Israel live in peace!

Psalm 129 – Persecute the Persecutors
A song to ascend

¹ They've persecuted me since my youth!
Let all Israel speak the truth:
² "Since the beginning we've faced discrimination.
Yet they failed in my subjugation!
³ They carved my back like a ploughed field,
with long deep wounds; I still didn't yield!
⁴ But The Lord, is righteous and absolute.

He breaks the chains of the wicked that persecute!
⁵ May the Zion haters be turned back!
Shame then, defeat them in their attack!
⁶ May they be like grass on a rooftop,
it withers and dies, when the growing stops!
⁷ Like weeds the reaper will ignore them.
So worthless, none will want to store them.
⁸ Let none that sees them say:
"Upon you, be the blessing of Yahweh!
May The Lord, bless you I pray!"

Psalm 130 – Desperate Cry
A song to ascend

¹ From the depths of my despair,
I cry Lord, "Are you there?"
² O Lord, hear my mercy pleas;
let your ears listen to me!
³ If you kept a record of all our iniquities,
who would ever then, be set free?
⁴ Yet, your forgiveness makes you, it is true!
So we love to serve, and worship you!
⁵ My whole being waits upon The Lord.
I put all my hope, in his Word.
⁶ I wait for The Lord,
more than watchmen wait for morning light,
I long for you, and watch for you, through the night!
⁷ The hope of The Lord, is in Israel!

His love will never fail.
⁸ He frees you from any jail!
He gives Israel redemption,
for all of their transgression!

Psalm 131 - My Humble Heart
A song to ascend by King David

¹ Lord, before you I humble my heart.
I let pride and arrogance depart.
I'm not interested in playing a big part,
or with complex subjects, that push me too far!
² In your peaceful presence, I wait humbly,
as, in a mother's arms, a child lies quietly.
So my heart is stilled within me.
³ Israel's hope is in God, for eternity!

Psalm 132 – Destiny and Desire
A song to ascend

¹ Lord, don't let David slip your mind.
He endured struggles of every kind!
² Lord, remember the promise he made, in your sight.
He vowed to Jacob's God, the God of Might!
³ He said, "I'll not return to my homestead.
I will not go to bed.

⁴ Sleep will not enter my eyes; all rest will be denied!
⁵ Until God's dwelling place is in my sight.
I need a home for Jacob's God; the God of Might!"
⁶ In Bethlehem, we heard, the Ark couldn't be found.
Yet, there it was at Jearim, safe and sound.
⁷ We said, "Let's go into The Lord's home.
Let's bow down and worship before his throne!"
⁸ Come Lord, come to your place of rest.
You and your Ark; will forever be blessed!
⁹ May your priests always do what is right.
Let all your people shout with joyful delight!
¹⁰ Don't reject your chosen king, Lord.
Honour your servant David,
you gave him your word.
¹¹ God gave David a sure oath,
he will not revoke or bemoan:
"One of your descendants will inherit your throne.
¹² If your sons keep my covenant commands,
they will always sit upon your throne."
¹³ The Lord, has chosen Zion, he has selected well.
It's his desired place to dwell.
¹⁴ I hear God speak,
"I will always live here and make it my own.
This is my desire, where I will sit upon my throne!
¹⁵ I will provide Zion with plenty and good.
Her poor will have satisfying food.
¹⁶ I will bless her priest with salvation.
Her people will always sing, in joyful celebration!
Shouting righteous declarations!
¹⁷ A great king will become, in David's son.

Here I will sustain my anointed one.
I will cover his enemies with shame.
Yet, his kingdom will prosper, thrive and remain!"

Psalm 133 – Peaceful Unity

A song to ascend by King David

[1] How good and wonderful is the harmony;
when God's people live together in unity!
[2] It's like precious anointing oil bestowed,
upon Aaron's head, down his beard it flows.
It drips down to the collar of his robes.
[3] This unity is like Mount Hermon dew.
It runs onto Mount Zion,
where God's blessings breakthrough.
The blessings are found in life, as it always continues!

Psalm 134 - The Night of Praise

A song to ascend

[1] Come, rejoice before The Lord, you servants always!
Serve in the house of God, with a night of praise!
[2] In the safe place, pray with hands raised.
Come, bring The Lord, your praise!
[3] From Zion, may The Lord, bless your dedication!
For he is the Glory, Lord of all Creation!

Psalm 135 – Shout Hallelujah and Praise
A song to ascend

¹ To the God of greatness, shout hallelujah and praise!
All his servants, praise him always!
² You who serve in the house of The Lord,
you who work within his court.
³ Praise The Lord, he's good all the time!
Praise his name in song, for he is kind.
⁴ He chose Jacob, for his own pleasure,
and Israel, as his special treasure.
⁵ I know that our God is great!
He's greater than false gods that try to imitate!
⁶ He does whatever he pleases, through all creation,
in the deepest seas and the greatest ocean!
⁷ From the ends of the earth, he makes clouds rise.
He sends lightning and rain to fill the skies.
From his storehouse comes a windy surprise!
⁸ In Egypt, he struck down the first born,
both man and beast, he did scorn!
⁹ He performed, signs and wonders, as demonstration.
He punished the Pharaoh administration,
without reservation!
¹⁰ He destroyed many, many nations.
Their mighty kings faced assassination!
¹¹ Like Sihon, king of the Amorites,
and Og, king of Bashan
and all the kings of the Canaanites.
¹² He gave their land as imperative,
to the Israel nation, as their heritage.

¹³ O Lord God, you're our eternal proclamation!
Your fame, will remain, in every generation.
¹⁴ The Lord, gives his people vindication.
His servants receive his compassionate consideration.
¹⁵ Work, wealth and idols
are worshipped by the other nations.
They're fashioned by human formulation.
¹⁶ The idols have mouths, yet voices they cannot find.
They have two eyes, yet still they're blind!
¹⁷ They have ears, but are totally deaf.
In their mouths they have no breath!
¹⁸ The idols are all dead, just like their makers.
The makers are misled, like all who trust the fakers!
¹⁹ Israel, give The Lord, a praise declaration!
All you priests, praise The Lord, in celebration!
²⁰ Praise The Lord, all you Levites!
Praise him, all you that worship and delight!
²¹ Praise The Lord, on Zion's throne,
in Jerusalem, his home.
Praise The Lord!

Psalm 136 - His Love Endures For Eternity!

¹ Give thanks to The Lord, for he is good quality!
His love endures for eternity!
² Give thanks to God, over false gods and everything!
His love is everlasting!
³ Give thanks to, The Lord of lords!

His love will last forever more!
4 Praise the wonders, done by him only!
His love endures for eternity!
5 Praise the heavens, made by his understanding!
His love is never ending!
6 Praise the earth he built on the waters deep!
His mighty love will never cease!
7 Praise the one who made the heavenly lights!
His love endures outright, never lose the fight!
8 Praise the one who made the sun to rule the day!
His love will never fade away!
9 Praise the one who made the moon to rule the night!
His love endures outright, never lose the fight!
10 Praise him who killed Egypt's firstborn!
His love will never die and mourn!
11 Praise him who delivered Israel!
His love endures and never fails!
12 Praise him who saves,
with an outstretch arm and a hand of might!
His love endures outright, never lose the fight!
13 Praise him who split the Red Sea!
His love endures for eternity!
14 Praise him for leading Israel through!
His love will always pursue!
15 Praise him who drowned Pharaoh and his army!
His love endures for eternity!
16 Praise him who led his people,
through the desert hot!
His love will never stop!
17 Praise him who killed the mighty kings!

His love is everlasting!
¹⁸ Praise him who killed,
the mighty kings who stood in his way!
His love will never fade away!
¹⁹ He conquered Sihon, king of the Amorites!
His love endures outright, never lose the fight!
²⁰ He conquered Og, of Bashan, the giant king!
His love is everlasting!
²¹ He gave their land as a legacy!
His love endures for eternity!
²² He gave it to his people Israel!
His love endures and never fails!
²³ He remembered us when we were nothing!
His love is everlasting!
²⁴ He freed us from our enemies!
His love endures for eternity!
²⁵ He gives food to every creature!
His love will always endure!
²⁶ Give thanks to God in the heavens high!
His great love will never die!

His love endures forever

Psalm 137 - Captivity Song

[1] By the rivers of Babylon, we sat in captivity;
where we wept and remembered Zion city!
[2] In our defeat and disadvantage,
we hung our harps on willow branches!
[3] Our captors asked for songs.
They tormented, "A joyful song, we do long!
Sing a happy Zion song!"
[4] But how could we sing The Lord's song,
in a foreign place where we didn't belong?
[5] If I forget the Jerusalem name,
may I never make music again!
[6] Then much the same,
if I don't consider Jerusalem my highest gain,
may I never be able to sing again!
[7] Lord, remember the Edomite's declaration,
on the day of Jerusalem's capitulation,
"Destroy the city, down to its foundation!"
[8] Babylon, you will face annihilation!
Happy are those who payback with aggravation!
They gain their appropriate compensation!
[9] Their babies' lives are their remuneration,
As they are smashed on the rocks of devastation!

Psalm 138 – Thanksgiving Prayer
By King David

¹ Thank you Lord, my whole heart is raised.
Before the angels, I will sing your praise!
² I bow down towards your holy temple
and praise your name.
For your faithfulness and love,
always remain the same.
You have raised your holy Word,
that it exceeds your fame!
³ When I called, you answered me hence,
with your strength, you gave me strength!
⁴ O Lord,
all the kings of the earth will give you praise,
when they hear your life transforming ways.
⁵ O Lord, may they sing your wonderful story.
Let them sing of your great glory!
⁶ Even though The Lord, is lifted high,
you care for the lowly and deprived.
From you the proud can never hide!
⁷ When I walk through trouble and devastation,
you are my salvation, my life's preservation.
You oppose my enemy aggravation!
Your power is my emancipation!
⁸ The Lord, gives me his vindication.
His love lasts for the endless duration.
Do not abandon your loving creation!

Psalm 139 - Intimate With Me
For public worship – A poetic song by King David

[1] O Lord, you have searched me.
You know me intimately!
[2] You know when I sit and when I rise;
You hear my thoughts from your heavenly skies.
My every thought you define,
before entering my mind.
[3] You know when I work and when I rest.
You're intimate with my progress.
[4] Before I even speak out,
you know what I'll talk about.
[5] You're on my every side, giving me attention.
Your mighty power gives me protection!
[6] Your intimate knowledge of me
is deeper than my limitation.
It is way beyond my imagination and realisation!
[7] Where can I go to escape your face?
Is there such a thing as a 'God free space'?
[8] You are there, if I go to the place of the dead!
You are there, if I go to heaven instead!
[9] You are there, if I fly into the morning sunrise!
You are there, if I settle on the sunset side!
[10] Wherever I go, your hand will be my guide;
your strength will help me by your side.
[11] I could ask darkness to hide me from your sight?
Maybe the light, around me could turn to night?
[12] Yet, even in darkness you still have sight.
Day and night, they're just as bright!

To you, darkness is as light!
¹³ You made my inside and outside bloom.
You knit me together in my mother's womb.
¹⁴ I am fearfully and wonderfully made,
 so I give you all the praise!
With your strange and wonderful ways,
my heart is truly amazed!

¹⁵ When my bones were in construction,
the womb formed me by your instruction.
Made from your creation reproduction!
¹⁶ You saw my unformed body with your eyes.
You recorded the days I would survive.
You did it all before I was alive!
¹⁷ O God, how precious are your thoughts of me.
Too many to count, such a vast quantity!
¹⁸ If I could count them, they are more;
than the grains of sand on the shore.
You are with me at dawn to reassure!
¹⁹ O God, why aren't the haters all deceased?
How I wish that the wicked would leave me in peace!
²⁰ See how they blaspheme your sacred name!
They speak evil against you, but all in vain!

²¹ O Lord, how I hate the haters that hate you!
I despise the despisers that rise against you too!
²² I hate their hatred with utter disgust!
Your enemies are my enemy; that is sussed!
²³ Search me, O God and know my heart.
Try me and know my anxious part.
²⁴ See if there be any hurtful way I've gone astray.
Then lead me in the everlasting way!

Psalm 140 - Petition for Protection

For public worship – A poetic song by King David

¹ From the haters, give me salvation!
From the violence, give me protection!
² They devise evil plans in their hearts.
Every day they argue and make war start!
³ These snakes are known for their poisonous words.
Their sharp, toxic tongues, just want to be heard!
They're so disturbed!
(Pause in his presence)

⁴ Lord, keep me safe from the hateful infection.
From the violence, give me protection!
They make wicked plans for my deception!
⁵ Along my path, their trap is set.
They sit in ambush with their net!
(Pause in his presence)

⁶ I say to my God, "You're my Lord, Adonai!"
Hear, O Lord, my mercy cry.
⁷ Sovereign Lord, my strong defender and shield,
you protect my head on the battle field!
⁸ Don't let the wicked triumph over me.
Foil their spiteful strategy,
or they become even more cocky!
(Pause in his presence)

⁹ Those who surround me proudly rear their heads;
may they be consumed, by their own threats!
¹⁰ May they be covered with red-hot coal!
Let them fall into the deepest, inescapable hole!
¹¹ Crush the triumphs,
of those that make false accusation!
May evil push the haters to annihilation!
¹² O Lord, you protect the poor in persecution.
You secure justice for the needy in destitution.
¹³ Surely the righteous will praise your name.
They will live in your presence and there remain!

Sovereign Lord my strong defender and shield, you protect my head on the battle field!

Psalm 141 - An Evening Sacrifice
A poetic song by King David

¹ O Lord, hear my plea, please come quickly.
When I call, you listen and come to me!
² May my prayer be as a scented delight!
Let my raised hands be as an evening sacrifice.
³ O Lord, set a guard over my lips.
Prevent me from speaking amiss.
⁴ Protect my heart from evil temptation.
Save me from the wicked population,
involved in evil occupation.
Steer me in the direction, away from sinful recreation!
⁵ It's a kind thing, when the upright person strikes,
when they rebuke my mistake, it's a delight.
For my prayer is against the evil seen in my sight!
⁶ Their leaders will be thrown from a clifftop height.
Then people will know that my words were right!
⁷ As a plough leaves the earth in tatters,
so their bones will be shattered!
At the mouth of hell, they will be scattered!
⁸ O Sovereign Lord, in you I trust and rely.
I seek your protection, don't let me die!
⁹ Keep me safe, in your care,
safe from the wicked hater's snare!
¹⁰ Let them all fall into their own traps,
while I escape without a scratch!

Psalm 142 -Desperation Prayer

A reflective poem, of David –
Composed when he was in the cave

¹ I loudly shout to The Lord, so worthy.
I lift my voice and beg, "Lord, show me mercy!"
² Before God, I moan and shout!
I pour my troubled heart out!
³ When I had doubt, I nearly gave up in desperation.
Yet, you guide me on my destination,
avoiding enemy traps and exploitation!
⁴ In my state of rejection; I look in every direction.
I see no one giving me protection.
⁵ I cry to you Lord, for your aid,
for you are my protector that saves.
You are my life's crusade; you are my upgrade!
⁶ Hear my heart cry for your care,
for I am crushed and in despair!
Please save me from the haters,
for they are so much greater!
⁷ Free me from my prison pain,
that I may praise your name!
Then all the righteous celebrate,
when they see you're good and great!

Psalm 143 - Humility Prayer
A poetic song by King David –
Composed when he was chased by Absalom

¹ O Lord, I cry out my prayer, in humility!
In your righteousness, hear my plea!
Show me your faithful mercy!
² Don't summon me to be judged!
For in your presence, no one is righteous.
³ My enemies chased and have crushed,
my life into dust.
Into the darkest prison, I am thrust!
Like many before, I'm dead and hushed!
⁴ My spirit is mentally depressed!
My heart struggles, shocked and stressed!
⁵ I remember your miracles of by-gone-days.
I contemplate your glorious, wonderful ways.
⁶ I lift up my hands to you in prayer.
Like dry ground my soul thirsts for your care.
(Pause in his presence)

⁷ O Lord, answer me in my depression and dread.
Don't hide yourself from me instead.
If you leave me now, I'll end up dead!
⁸ Let each new dawn
bring your unfailing love revelation.
For I trust in your salvation.
As you hear my prayer, show me your destination!
⁹ O Lord, I go to you for protection.

Rescue me from my enemy deception!
¹⁰ O God, show me your bidding, I pray.
Let your Spirit guide me along the safe way!
¹¹ For your name's sake, Lord, preserve my life!
Let your goodness deliver me from trouble and strife!
¹² Through your unfailing love, my enemies,
you will silence.
As I am you servant, you destroy my foes in violence!

Psalm 144 – Thanks For Redeeming Me
A poetic song by King David –
Composed when he stood before Goliath

¹ Praise God, my protector so secure.
He trains my hand for battle, prepares me for war.
² He's my shelter of love, my faith fortress.
I hide in his refuge,
while my enemies he does supress.
³ Lord, what is it that you care about us?
What are your intentions?
We are vulnerable human beings,
yet, you give us your attention!
⁴ For man, is just like the wind that blows.
Our days are like a passing shadow.
⁵ Lord, rip open the skies and come down here.
When you touch the mountains,
you make smoke appear.
⁶ Scatter your enemies with your lightning flash.

Shoot your fiery arrows and see them dash!
You attack from the skies, they run for their lives!
⁷ Reach down your hand and give me assistance.
Rescue me from this consuming existence.
Save me from the alien resistance!
⁸ They're a bunch of lying cheats!
You can never trust their words of deceit!
⁹ O God, I will sing you a brand-new song!
I will play my harp and sing along!
¹⁰ You give kings the victory.
Your servant David, you do set free!
¹¹ Save me; from the enemy fire.
Rescue me, from the alien occupier.
Their all nothing but a bunch of liars!
¹² May our young sons be like strong vegetation!
Let our daughters have beauty fashioned
like a royal habitation.
¹³ Fill our barns with food to overflowing.
Let the sheep in the field
produce thousands of offspring.
¹⁴ May our cattle reproduce and multiply.
Let our strong walls keep the peace and hear no cries!
¹⁵ We have such delight, when these blessings accord!
Blessed are the people, whose God is The Lord!

Psalm 145 - God's Greatness

A poetic song of praise by King David

¹ My God and King, I give you my exaltation!
I will always praise you name, in great appreciation!
² Every day I lift up and praise your name,
I thank you for everything,
and this will always remain!
³ Great is The Lord, and most worthy of praise!
He's so beyond our understanding, we are amazed!
⁴ Your works will be praised,
from generation to generation.
Your mighty acts and greatness;
will be your declaration.
⁵ They will speak of your majestic glorification.
Your wonderful deeds will be my meditation.
⁶ Everyone everywhere,
talks about your great sensations!
Your awesome deeds will be my proclamation!
⁷ They celebrate your abundant goodness.
They sing with joy of your righteousness.
⁸ The Lord, is compassionate and full of grace.
He is rich in love and slow to rage.
⁹ The Lord, is good to every nation.
He shows compassion on all creation.
¹⁰ Everything you have made, will give you praise.
All your people thank you always.
¹¹ They will speak of your kingdom glory.
They will tell of your mighty story.
¹² Then all people may know your mighty acts done.

They will see the glorious splendour of your kingdom.
¹³ You're our Everlasting King, you reign eternal!
The Lord's promises are faithful,
all he does is merciful.
¹⁴ For all who fall; he will sustain.
He lifts up all who bow down in shame.
¹⁵ Everyone looks and keeps you in their sight.
You feed them all when the time is right.
¹⁶ Everything living sees your action,
you provide their needs of satisfaction.
¹⁷ The Lord is righteous in all his ways,
and faithful in all he does and says.
¹⁸ O Lord, you're close to all who call to you.
That's especially so, when their hearts are true.
¹⁹ He fulfils the desires of all,
who stand in fear and awe.
He saves all who call.
²⁰ To all, that love him, he gives protection.
To the wicked he gives, total destruction.
²¹ My lips, will always praise The Lord!
Let every creature praise his holy name
for ever and ever more!

My lips will always praise the Lord!

Psalm 146 – Praise Our True Saviour

A poetic Psalm by Haggai and Zechariah

[1] The name of The Lord, be praised!
I praise The Lord, with my soul raised!
[2] I will praise The Lord all my life!
I praise my God, while I'm alive!
[3] Don't ever put your trust in human leadership,
for no man will ever save you from the pit!
[4] They return to the ground, when their spirit departs,
on the day they die; their plans fall apart!
[5] The God of Jacob, gives help and blessings.
Their hope is in The Lord, God Everlasting!
He's the heavens and earth's Creator.
[6] All the seas and life that swim, within,
he is the Maker.
His faith is always greater!
[7] The oppressed are justified!
The hungry are satisfied!
The prisoners are all untied!
[8] The blind have sight regained!
He restores those bent down in shame!
He loves those who honour his name!
The Lord, guards the alien with fortification.
[9] He helps widows and orphans with sustentation
and preservation.
The wicked face his frustration and ruination!
[10] The Lord reigns for time duration!
Zion's God, rules through all generations!
Hallelujah! Praise God, in acclamation!

Psalm 147
We Praise El Shaddai (God Almighty)

[1] Hallelujah! Praise God, El Shaddai!
It is good to sing praise, to God Most High!
We have pleasure, in great measure,
praising El Shaddai!
[2] The Lord, gives Jerusalem its restoration!
He provides the exiles repatriation!
[3] He heals every broken heart.
He cares for their cuts and scars.
[4] He decides the number of stars
and names them to tell them apart.
[5] Great is our Lord, El Shaddai.
His wisdom is too great to specify.
[6] God sustains the humble, it's a must!
The wicked he crushes into the dust!
[7] Sing to The Lord, with songs of praise!
On the harp, praise God always!
[8] He spreads his clouds throughout the sky.
The earth needs rain, so he provides,
then grows the grass on every hillside.
[9] Every beast, he feeds them all.
He feeds young ravens, when they call.
[10] He takes no pleasure in the strength of a horse.
He has no delight in the number of legs,
in his warrior force!
[11] The Lord delights in those who fear him and avail.
Those who put their hope in his love that never fails.
[12] Jerusalem, lift your praise to El Shaddai!

O Zion, worship, The Lord Adonai!
¹³ He strengthens the bars of your gates.
Your inhabitants receive blessings, as God allocates.
¹⁴ He keeps your borders safe and sound.
He pleases you, with the best crop in the ground.
¹⁵ To the earth, he gives his instruction.
The command he gives, is swiftly done.
¹⁶ Like a woollen blanket, he spreads the snow.
He scatters a dusting of frost, just so.
¹⁷ Hail like rocks, he does throw.
No one can stand his icy blow!
¹⁸ When he speaks his word, the ice will go.
As the spring winds blow,
the frozen streams will flow.
¹⁹ He gives his people his Word, without fail.
He gives instruction and laws to Israel.
²⁰ He does this for no other nation tribe.
For his laws, they all do deny!
Hallelujah! Give praise to El Shaddai!

Psalm 148 – Let The Universe Praise God

¹ Hallelujah! Praise The Lord, with gratification!
Fill the skies with his praise in acclamation!
Praise him in his heavenly glorification!
² Praise him, all you angels of God!
Make some noise, you angelic squad!
³ Praise him, you moon and sun!

Praise him, you shining stars, every single one!
4 Praise him, in the heavens so high!
Praise him, all you waters above the sky!
5 Praise him, O universe with your booming thunder!
For he commanded and made your glorious wonder!
6 By his galactic command,
he established it by his hand.
All the planets understand; they will forever stand!
7 Let the earth join in with the praise celebration!
You great sea creatures deep, join the exaltation!
8 All you lightning, hail, clouds and snow.
And make it so, you strong winds that obey and blow.
9 Praise him, you hills and mountains high!
Praise him, you trees and forests, shout your cry!
10 Praise him, all you beasts, both tame and wild!
Praise him, all you kinds of birds and reptiles!
11 Praise him, you kings and queens of earthly nations!
Praise him, you princes and princesses,
who rule as your designation!
12 Praise him, men and women in their youth!
Praise him, old people and children too!
13 Come all, join together without delays!
The name of The Lord, is the one to praise!
For his name is the only one we raise!
Above the heavens, is his glorious blaze!
14 He has given strength to his nation.
So his people praise him in exaltation!
The Israelites, never turn away in separation!
Hallelujah! Praise The Lord, in acclamation!

Psalm 149
Join The Praise Throng, Where You Belong!

¹ Hallelujah! Praise The Lord, in song!
Sing to The Lord, a brand new song!
Praise in the assembled faithful throng!
² Let Israel rejoice in the Maker of everything.
Let the people of Zion, have joy in their King.
³ Let's praise his name with dancing.
Play the harp and drums, keep your praise advancing!
⁴ For The Lord, takes delight in the faithful of Zion.
He blesses the humble with a crown of triumph!
⁵ Let God's people rejoice in victory!
Hear them joyfully, sing nocturnally.
⁶ May the praise of God, be on their lips,
with a double-edged sword, held in their grip!
⁷ They will bring vengeance upon the nations.
They will punish the generations!
⁸ They will bind their kings in chains
Their leaders in shackles will remain!
⁹ They punish the nations, following God's command.
They give God the glory in the victory stand!
Hallelujah! Praise The Lord; strike up the band!

Psalm 150 – Hallelujah! Praise The Lord!

¹ Hallelujah! Praise The Lord in his sanctuary!
Hallelujah! Praise The Lord in his mighty heavenlies!
² For his mighty deeds, we give him praise!
Praise him for his absolute great ways!
³ Praise him with the trumpet sound!
Praise him with all instruments found!
⁴ Praise him on guitar and drums to astound!
Praise him like you know no bounds!
⁵ Praise him as the cymbal clash resounds!
⁶ Praise The Lord, all you creatures living!
Hallelujah! Praise The Lord, with thanksgiving!

Psalm 74:13

You brought Forth fountains from the rock The mighty flowing rivers you did block

Request from the author

I do hope that you enjoyed reading this book and that
it gave you as much pleasure,
as it was for me writing it.

**Please review this book on Amazon and
Goodreads – Thank you!**

**Brendan Conboy has an active
writing and speaking
MINISTRY for GOD
and is looking forward to
hearing from you**

Contact Brendan at the following:
Email – bmconboy@gmail.com
Phone - +44 (0)1453 731008
Mobile – 07980 404873
www.brendanconboy.co.uk

**The following pages contain information
about Brendan's book titles (Bibliography).**

The Golden Thread – Biography
A true story of fear, forgiveness and faith
First published – 1ˢᵗ September 2015

Brendan Conboy grew up in fear and confusion, struggling with many personal issues. These experiences formed a foundation which could have ended in disaster, but instead, became the motivator to want to make a positive difference.

Issues – Teen / YA Fiction
We all have issues… Can a bully change?
First published – 23ʳᵈ January 2019

Marcus Daniel was a caring, intelligent, larger than average ten year old. His parents changed and then so did he. Now Marcus is thirteen years old and a spiteful bully, full of anger, rage and pain. His actions have changed others. Will the fear, pain and rage win?

My Foundation for Life – Semi Biog / Scriptural Teaching
14 underpinning and impacting scriptures
First published – 19th February 2019

What is it that makes some of us more resilient than others? I am sure that psychologists will have several long-winded explanations to answer this question, but I believe that we can increase our resilience by building our lives on a foundation of truth

Rhyme Time – Poetry
Poems with a message for you to read.
Poems of truth that plant a seed.
First published – 13th November 2020

The Invasion of the MIMICS
Science Fiction / Dystopian / Fantasy
They're already here... Invading your country...
Dwelling in your home... Living in your body!
First published – 21st October 2020

Climate change had been predicted long ago, but not one person could foresee the events that had unfolded. Humanity is defeated, civilization lost, all hope has gone. Enlightenment is the new belief, but there are those that refuse to believe.

The Land of Make Believe – Children's fantasy in rhyme
Based on the story of doubting Thomas
First published – June 2021

Look out for

The LEGACY of the MIMICS

www.ingramcontent.com/pod-product-compliance
Lightning Source LLC
Chambersburg PA
CBHW071726080526
44588CB00013B/1920